SIMPLY
MANAGING

Other Books by Henry Mintzberg

SIMPLY MANAGING

What Managers Do—
And Can Do Better

HENRY MINTZBERG

BK

Berrett–Koehler Publishers, Inc.
San Francisco
a BK Business book

Berrett-Koehler Publishers, Inc.
235 Montgomery Street, Suite 650
San Francisco, CA 94104-2916
Tel: (415) 288-0260   Fax: (415) 362-2512   www.bkconnection.com

Ordering Information

Quantity sales. Special discounts are available on quantity purchases by corporations, associations, and others. For details, contact the "Special Sales Department" at the Berrett-Koehler address above.

Individual sales. Berrett-Koehler publications are available through most bookstores. They can also be ordered directly from Berrett-Koehler: Tel: (800) 929-2929; Fax: (802) 864-7626; www.bkconnection.com

Orders for college textbook/course adoption use. Please contact Berrett-Koehler: Tel: (800) 929-2929; Fax: (802) 864-7626.

Orders by U.S. trade bookstores and wholesalers. Please contact Ingram Publisher Services, Tel: (800) 509-4887; Fax: (800) 838-1149; E-mail: customer.service@ ingrampublisherservices.com; or visit www.ingrampublisherservices.com/Ordering for details about electronic ordering.

Berrett-Koehler and the BK logo are registered trademarks of Berrett-Koehler Publishers, Inc.

Printed in the United States of America

Berrett-Koehler books are printed on long-lasting acid-free paper. When it is available, we choose paper that has been manufactured by environmentally responsible processes. These may include using trees grown in sustainable forests, incorporating recycled paper, minimizing chlorine in bleaching, or recycling the energy produced at the paper mill.

Production Management: **Michael Bass Associates**
Cover Design: Stephen Taylor, Heat Design
Author Photo: Owen Egan 2010

Library of Congress Cataloging-in-Publication Data
Mintzberg, Henry.
    Simply managing : what managers do and can do better / Henry Mintzberg.
        pages   cm. — (A BK business book)
    This is a substantially condensed and somewhat revised version of the author's title, Managing, published in 2009.
    Includes bibliographical references and index.
    ISBN 978-1-60994-923-5 (pbk. : alk. paper)
    1. Management. I. Title.
    HD31.M45718 2013
    658—dc23
                                                                                    2013016851

First Edition
18   17   16   15   14   13   10   9   8   7   6   5   4   3   2   1

Contents

Welcome to
Simply Managing

This book is written for practicing managers, about their practice of management, and for the many other people influenced by and interested in that practice. It may be especially helpful for new managers befuddled by this strange new world of managing. *Simply Managing* is a substantially condensed and somewhat revised version of my book *Managing* (2009), to focus on its essence for busy readers.

The boldface sentences summarize the key points in this book and so serve as a running commentary throughout. (There are no chapter summaries; I believe that these sentences do that job more effectively.) Use them if you are the harried manager described in Chapter 2, and probe around them if you wish to be the reflective manager prescribed in Chapter 5. To help, here is an overview of the six chapters:

- *Chapter 1* opens things up by questioning a number of common **myths** about managing—for example, that leadership is more important than management. This chapter is short but necessary for what follows, so please read it!

- *Chapter 2* describes the **relentless pressures** on managers—the hectic pace, the interruptions, the disorder that has to be ordered, and more. Slow down and have a look—you may find some surprises.

- *Chapter 3* addresses the basic content of the job—**what managers do and why.** Managing is described as happening on three "planes": through information, with people, and for action. The boldface sentences may come in especially handy here.

- *Chapter 4* considers the untold **varieties** of managing: in different cultures; at different levels of the hierarchy; practiced as art, craft, and science; and so on. The boldface sentences can direct you to some conclusions you may not be expecting.

- *Chapter 5* goes to the heart of what makes managing difficult: the **conundrums** that force every manager to walk on all kinds of tightropes concurrently. For example: How to connect in a job that is intrinsically disconnected? How to maintain confidence without becoming arrogant? I believe this is the most important chapter of the book: read it to face the unresolvable aspects of the job, rather than trying to resolve them.

- *Chapter 6* looks at what makes managers **effective.** Don't expect the usual exhortations here. Appreciate, instead, that managers should be selected for their flaws as well as their strengths (and who is to know these better than the people they have managed), that the best managers often prove to be clearheaded and emotionally healthy, and more. Enough of heroic leadership—it's time for engaging management!

1 Managing Beyond the Myths

What management is and isn't

A half century ago Peter Drucker (1954) put management on the map. Leadership has since pushed it off the map. We are now inundated with great stories about the grand successes and even grander failures of great leaders, but we have yet to come to grips with the realities of being a manager.

This is a book about managing, simply managing—even if the job is not simple. It considers the characteristics, contents, and varieties of the job, as well as the conundrums faced by managers, and how they become effective. My objective is straightforward. Managing is important for anyone affected by its practice, which means not just managers, but everyone. We all need to understand it better, in order that it be practiced better. Some of the questions addressed in the book include these:

- Are managers too busy managing?
- Is leadership really separate from management?
- Is the Internet hindering managers as it helps them?

- How are managers to connect when the very nature of their job disconnects them from what they are managing?
- Where has all the judgment gone?

For years I have been asking groups of people in this job, "What happened the day you became a manager? Were you offered any guidance at all?" The response has almost always been the same: puzzled looks, then shrugs. You are supposed to figure it out for yourself, like sex, I suppose, usually with equally embarrassing initial consequences. Yesterday you were playing the flute or doing surgery; today you find yourself managing people who are doing these things. Everything has changed, yet you are on your own, confused and overwhelmed. This book is meant to help, not by offering easy answers—there are none—but by encouraging deeper understanding.

SOME SOBERING REALITY

In the late 1960s, for my doctoral dissertation, I observed five managers during one week each. The result was my first book, *The Nature of Managerial Work* (1973). In the 1990s, I revisited that work, spending a day observing each of 29 managers in a variety of settings—business, government, health care, NGOs—at senior, middle, and operating levels, in organizations ranging from 18 to 800,000 employees (see Figure 1). The insights were revealing, and sobering. (Full descriptions of these days, and what I learned from them, can be found on www.mintzberg–managing .com.) I used these findings in my 2009 book *Managing.* **Simply Managing is a shortened version of *Managing,* reduced to**

its essence for managers and everyone else interested in management. Here is some of that sobering reality.

"Top" managers take the long view, see the "big picture"; "lower"-level managers deal with the narrower, immediate ⋈ *things. So why was Gord Irwin, front country manager of the Banff National Park in Canada, so concerned with the environmental consequences of a parking lot expansion at a ski hill, while back in Ottawa, Norman Inkster, commissioner of the whole Royal Canadian Mounted Police, was watching clips of last night's television news to head off embarrassing questions to his minister in Parliament that day?*

And why was Jacques Benz, director-general of GSI, a high-technology company in Paris, sitting in on a meeting about a customer's project? He was a senior manager, after all. Shouldn't he have been back in his office developing grand strategies? Paul Gilding, executive director of Greenpeace International, was trying to do just that, with considerable frustration. Who had it right?

One of the managers I studied was Alan Whelan in Global Computing and Electronics at BT in the U.K. Because he was a sales manager, you might have expected him to have been meeting customers, or at least working with his people to help them sell to customers. On this day, Alan was selling, all right, but to an executive of his own company, who was reluctant to sign off on his biggest contract. To use the conventional words of managing, was Alan planning, organizing, commanding, coordinating, or controlling?

FIGURE 1   **The Twenty-Nine Managers Observed***

	BUSINESS	GOVERNMENT
Management Overall ("Top")	*John Cleghorn* CEO Royal Bank of Canada	*John Tate* Deputy Minister, Canadian Department of Justice (Ottawa)
	Jacques Benz Director-General, GSI (Paris)	*Norm Inkster* Commissioner, Royal Canadian Mounted Police (RCMP, Ottawa)
	Carol Haslam Managing Director, Hawkshead Ltd. (film company, London)	
	Max Mintzberg Co-president, The Telephone Booth (retail chain, Montreal)	
Management in Between ("Middle")	*Brian Adams* Director, Global Express, Canadair (Bombardier, Montreal)	*Glen Rivard* General Counsel, Family and Youth Law, Canadian Department of Justice (Ottawa)
	Alan Whelan Sales Manager, Global Computing and Electronics Sector, BT (London)	*Doug Ward* Director of Programming CBC Radio (Ottawa)
		Allen Burchill Commanding Officer, "H" Division, RCMP (Halifax)
		Sandra Davis Regional Director-General, Parks Canada (Calgary)
		Charlie Zinkan Superintendent Banff National Park (Alberta)
Management at the Base ("Bottom")		*Gordon Irwin* Front Country Manager, Banff National Park (Alberta)
		Ralph Humble Commander, New Minas Detachment, RCMP (Nova Scotia)

*Note: Full descriptions of these days, with interpretations, can be found on www.mintzberg-managing.com.

HEALTH CARE	PLURAL SECTOR
Sir Duncan Nichol CEO, National Health Service of England (NHS, London)	*Paul Gilding* Executive Director, Greenpeace International (Amsterdam)
"Marc" Hospital Executive Director (Quebec)	*Dr. Rony Brauman* Président Médécins sans frontiers (Paris)
	Catherine Joint-Dieterle Conservateur en chef, Musée de la mode et de la costume (Paris)
	Bramwell Tovey Conductor, Winnipeg Symphony Orchestra
Peter Coe District General Manager (NHS, North Hertfordshire)	*Paul Hohnen* Director Toxic Trade, Forests, Economic and Political Units, Greenpeace International (Amsterdam)
Ann Sheen Director of Nursing Services, (NHS, Reading Hospitals)	*Abbas Gullet* Head of Subdelegation, International Red Cross Federation (N'gara, Tanzania)
Dr. Michael Thick Liver Transplant Surgeon St. Mary's Hospital (NHS, London)	*Stephen Omollo* Manager, Benac and Lukole Camps, International Red Cross Federation (N'gara, Tanzania)
Dr. Stewart Webb Clinical Director (Geriatrics), St. Charles Hospital (NHS, London)	
Fabienne Lavoie Head Nurse, 4 Northwest, Jewish General Hospital (Montreal)	

Fabienne Lavoie, head nurse on 4 Northwest, a pre- and post-operation surgical ward in a Montreal hospital, was working from 7:20 a.m. to 6:45 p.m. at a pace that exhausted this observer. At one point, in the space of a few minutes, she was discussing a dressing with a surgeon, putting through a patient's hospital card, rearranging her scheduling board, speaking with someone in reception, checking on a patient who had a fever, calling to fill in a vacancy, discussing some medication, and chatting with a patient's relative. Is managing supposed to be that hectic?

Finally, what about the famous metaphor of the manager as orchestra conductor, magnificently in charge so that the whole team can make beautiful music together? Bramwell Tovey of the Winnipeg Symphony Orchestra stepped off his podium to talk about the job. "The hard part," he said, "is the rehearsal process," not the performance. That's less grand. And how about being in charge? "You have to subordinate yourself to the composer," he said. So, does the orchestra "director" actually direct the orchestra—exercise that famous leadership? "We never talk about 'the relationship.'" So much for that metaphor.

Before proceeding, it will be helpful to revisit three other prominent myths that get in the way of seeing managing for what it is: somehow separate from leadership; a science, or at least a profession; and that managers, like everyone else, live in times of great change.

ENOUGH LEADERSHIP— TIME FOR "COMMUNITYSHIP"

It has become fashionable to distinguish leaders from managers. One does the right things, copes with change; the other does things right, copes with complexity (Bennis 1989; Kotter 1990; Zaleznik 1977). So tell me, who were the leaders and who the managers in the examples just mentioned? Was Alan Whelan merely managing at BT and Bramwell Tovey merely leading—on, and off, the podium? Was Jacques Benz of GSI doing the right things or doing things right?

How would you like to be managed by someone who doesn't lead? That could be dispiriting. Well, then, why would you want to be led by someone who doesn't manage? That could be disengaging: how are such "leaders" to know what is going on? As Jim March of the Stanford Business School put it: "Leadership involves plumbing as well as poetry" (in Augier 2004:173).

I observed John Cleghorn, chairman of the Royal Bank of Canada. He developed a reputation in his company for calling the office on his way to the airport to report a broken ATM machine, and such things. This bank has thousands of such machines. Was John micromanaging? Maybe he was setting an example that others should follow: keep your eyes open for such problems.

In fact, today we should be more worried about "macroleading"—from people in senior positions who try to manage by remote control, disconnected from everything except "the big picture." It has become popular to talk about us being overmanaged and underled. I believe **we are now overled and undermanaged.**

Instead of distinguishing leaders from managers, we should be seeing managers *as* leaders, and leadership as management practiced well.

Moreover, leadership focuses on the individual, whereas **this book sees managing together with leadership as naturally embedded in what can be called** *communityship.*

MANAGEMENT AS A PRACTICE, NOT A PROFESSION

After years of seeking these Holy Grails, **it is time to recognize that managing is neither a science nor a profession.**

Certainly Not a Science

Science is about the development of systematic knowledge through research. That is hardly the purpose of management, which is about helping to get things done in organizations.

Management certainly *applies* science: managers have to use all the knowledge they can get. But effective managing is more dependent on art and is especially rooted in craft. Art produces "insights," and "vision," based on intuition. (Peter Drucker wrote in 1954 that "the days of the 'intuitive' manager are numbered" [p. 93]. Sixty years later, we are still counting.) And craft is about learning from experience—working things out as the manager goes along.

Thus, as shown in Figure 2, managing can be seen as taking place within a triangle where art, craft, and the use of science meet. Art brings in the ideas and the integration; craft makes

FIGURE 2   **Managing as Art, Craft, Science**

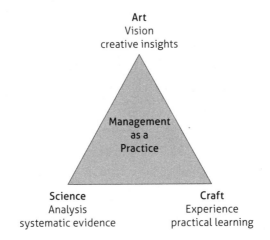

the connections, building on tangible experiences; and science provides the order, through systematic analysis of knowledge.

Managers deal with the messy stuff—the intractable problems, the complicated connections. This is what makes their work so fundamentally "soft" and why labels such as experience, intuition, judgment, and wisdom are so commonly needed to describe it. **Put together a good deal of craft with the right touch of art alongside some use of science, and you end up with a job that is above all a *practice,* learned through experience and rooted in context.** There is no "one best way" to manage; it depends on the situation.

Nor a Profession

Engineering, too, is not a science so much as a practice in its own right (Lewin 1979). But engineering uses a good deal of science, codified and certified as to its effectiveness. And so it can be called a profession, which means that it can be taught in advance of practice, out of context. In a sense, a bridge is a bridge, or at least steel is steel, even if its use has to be adapted to the circumstances at hand. The same can be said about medicine. But not about management. Little of its practice has been reliably codified, let alone certified as to its effectiveness. That is why Linda Hill, in her study of new managers, found that they "had to act as managers before they understood what the role was" (2003:45).

Ever since Frederick Taylor (1916) dubbed his work study method the "one best way," we have been searching for the Holy Grail of management in science and professionalism. Today that lives on in the easy formulas of so much of the popular literature, such as "strategic planning," and "shareholder value" (both oxymorons). Time and time again, the easy answers have failed.

In engineering and medicine, the trained expert can almost always outperform the layperson. Not so in management. Few of us would trust the intuitive engineer or physician, with no formal training. Yet we trust all kinds of managers who have never spent a day in a management classroom (and we have suspicions about many who have spent two years in an MBA programs [see my book *Managers, Not MBAs* [2004]).

The true professional knows better, as does the true scientist. But managers who believe they know better get in the way of their practice, because it has to be largely one of facilitation.

The manager, by the definition used here, is responsible for an organization or some unit in it. To use that old saying, managers get things done largely through other people. Managers have to know a lot, especially about their specific contexts, and they have to make decisions based on that knowledge. But, especially in large organizations and those concerned with "knowledge work," **the manager has to help bring out the best in other people, so that they can know better, decide better, and act better.**

MANAGING'S NOT CHANGING

This book draws on research from deep in the last century into our new millennium. My own twenty-nine days of observation took place in the 1990s. Books these days are not supposed to do such things—they are expected to be terribly up-to-date.

Let's try the reverse: terribly up-to-date can get in the way. We risk being mesmerized by the present and biased by the stories we "know" all too well. A little time between us and events can be a good thing.

Attend some speech on management. It is likely to begin with the claim that "we live in times of great change"—a mantra of so many managers. As you hear this, look at the clothes you are wearing. Notice the buttons, and ask yourself why, if we really live in times of great change, we are still buttoning buttons? Indeed, how come you drove to that speech in a car powered by an internal combustion four-cycle engine? Wasn't that used in the Model T Ford?

Why didn't you notice those buttons when you dressed this morning or that old technology when you drove to work? After all, when you arrived there, you did notice some change in the operating system of your computer. **The fact is that we only notice what is changing. And most things are not.** Information technology has been changing; we all notice that. Same with the economy of late. How about managing?

"For all the fashionable hype about leadership, it is unfashionable management that is being practiced and its fundamental characteristics have not changed" (Hales 2001:54). Managers deal with different issues as time moves forward, but not with different managing. If you doubt this, rent a good old movie about people managing a business or a war. Or look at the examples from the 1990s presented earlier in this chapter: did any of these strike you as out of date?

In this book, I draw on many years of research about managing, some of it going back almost a century. I do this simply because I wish to use the best insight we have, and, as you shall see, some of the oldest are among the best. Managing is managing.

As I hope has become evident in this opening chapter, I have written this book not to reinforce conventional wisdom—to add to all that stuffy managerial correctness—but to open up perspectives, so that we can all probe, ponder, and wonder about managing. I don't want you to leave this book knowing. I want you to leave it, as I do, imagining, reflecting, questioning. **Managers are only as good as their ability to work things out thoughtfully in their own way.** As you will see in Chapter 5, this is a job of paradoxes, dilemmas, and mysteries that cannot be resolved. The only guaranteed result of any formula for managing is failure (including this one of course).

So off we go, to the delights, duties, and distresses of the ancient and contemporary practice of managing.

2 Managing Relentlessly

The pressures of managerial work

Have a look at the popular images of managing—that conductor on the podium, those executives sitting at desks in *New Yorker* cartoons—and you get one impression of the job: well ordered, carefully controlled. Watch some managers at work and you will likely find something quite different: a hectic pace, lots of interruptions, more responding than initiating.

This chapter describes these and other dynamic characteristics of managing: how managers work, with whom, at what pace, and so on. Much of this evidence comes from the earlier studies, but more recent research suggests it is fully up-to-date (e.g., Hales 2001 and Tengblad 2006).

I first described these dynamics in my 1973 book. None of them could have come as a shock to anyone who ever spent a day in a managerial office, doing the job or observing it. Yet they struck a chord with many people—especially managers—perhaps because they challenged some of our most cherished myths about this job. Time and again, when I presented these conclusions to groups of managers, the common response was "You make me feel so good! While I thought that all those other managers were planning, organizing, coordinating, and controlling, I was constantly being interrupted, jumping from one issue to another, and trying to keep the lid on the chaos."

KNOWING—AND KNOWING

Why should there have been such reactions to what these managers doubtlessly knew already? My explanation is that, as human beings, we "know" in two different ways. Some things we know consciously, explicitly; we can verbalize them, often because we have so often heard or read about them. Other things we know viscerally, tacitly, based on our experience.

Surely we function best when these two kinds of knowing reinforce each other. In managing, they have often contradicted each other, requiring managers to live a set of myths—the folklore of managing as planning, organizing, and such, compared with the facts of daily managerial life. So **if we wish to make significant headway in improving the practice of managing, we need to bring the overt image in line with the covert reality.** That is the intention of this chapter, which describes the unrelenting pace of managing; the brevity, variety, discontinuity of its activities; the orientation to action; the favoring of informal and oral forms of communication; the lateral nature of managing (with colleagues and associates); and control in this job as implicit more than explicit.

Folklore: The manager is a reflective, systematic
            planner.

We have this common image of the manager, especially in senior
positions, sitting at a desk, thinking grand thoughts, making
great decisions, and, above all, systematically planning out the
future. There is a good deal of evidence about this, but not a
shred of it supports this image.

Fact: Study after study has shown that
        (a) managers work at an unrelenting pace;
        (b) their activities are characterized by
        brevity, variety, and fragmentation, and
        (c) they are strongly oriented to action.

The Pace

The reports on the hectic pace of managerial work have been
consistent, from foremen averaging one activity every forty-eight
seconds (Guest 1955–1956:478) and middle managers able to
work for at least a half hour without interruption only about
once every two days (Stewart 1967), to chief executives, half
of whose activities lasted less than nine minutes (Mintzberg
1973:33). "Over forty studies of managerial work dating back to
the 1950s have shown that 'executives just sort of dash around
all the time'" (McCall, Lombardo, and Morrison 1988:55).

In my first study, I noted that the work pace of the chief executives I observed was unrelenting. They met a steady stream of
callers and mail, from their arrival in the morning until their depar-
ture in the evening. Coffee breaks and lunches were inevitably

work related, and ever-present people in their organization were ready to usurp any free moment. As one put it to me, **the work of managing is "one damn thing after another."** The quantity of work to be done, or at least that managers choose to do during the day, is substantial, and after hours senior managers appear able to escape neither from a situation that recognizes the power of their position nor from their own predispositions to worry about current problems.

One reason for this has to be the inherently open-ended nature of the job. The manager is responsible for the success of the unit, yet there are no tangible mileposts where he or she can stop and say, "Now my job is finished." The engineer completes the design of a bridge on a particular day; the lawyer wins or loses a case at some moment in time. The manager, in contrast, must always keep going, never sure when success is truly assured or whether things might not come crashing down. As a result, **managing is a job with a perpetual preoccupation: the manager can never be free to forget the work, never has the pleasure of knowing, even temporarily, that there is nothing left to do.**

Variety and Interruption

Most work in society involves specialization and concentration. Engineers and programmers can spend months designing a machine or developing some software; salespeople can devote their working lives to selling one line of products. Managers can expect no such concentration of efforts.

The search for patterns in managerial work—during the day, across the week, over the year—has not found much, aside from a few budgeting cycles and the like. As Lee Iacocca commented about his highly visible CEO job: "Some days at Chrysler, I wouldn't have gotten up in the morning if I had known what was coming" (Iacocca, Taylor, and Bellis 1988). A surprising finding of my own initial study is that few of the chief executives' meetings and other contacts were held on a regularly scheduled basis. On average, thirteen out of fourteen were ad hoc.

What we find is a great deal of fragmentation in this work, and on top of that much interruption. Someone calls about a fire in a facility; a few e-mails are then scanned; an assistant comes in to inform about a challenge from a consumer group; then a retiring employee is ushered in to be presented with a plaque; after that it's more e-mails; and next it's off to a meeting about a bid for a large contract. And so it goes. Most surprising is that **the significant activities seem to be interspersed with the mundane in no particular pattern: hence, the manager must be prepared to shift moods quickly and frequently.**

Swedish economist Sune Carlson (1951) carried out an early empirical study of the managerial work of chief executives. He questioned why they did not free themselves from the interruptions by making better use of their secretaries and being more willing to delegate work. But he begged an important question: is brevity, variety, and fragmentation forced on the managers, or do they choose this pattern in their work? My answer is yes—both times, especially the second.

The five chief executives of my early study appeared to be properly protected by their secretaries, and there was no reason to believe that they were inferior delegators. Instead, they sometimes preferred interruption and denied themselves free time.

For example, they—not the other parties—terminated many of their meetings and telephone calls, and they themselves often interrupted quiet desk work to place phone calls or to request that people come by. One chief executive located his desk so that he looked down a long hallway. The door was usually open, and his reports were continually coming into his office.

Why this preference for interruption? **To some extent, managers tolerate interruptions because they do not wish to discourage the flow of current information.** Moreover, many become accustomed to variety in their work, and so boredom develops easily.

More to the point, however, **managers seem to become conditioned by their workload: they develop a sensitive appreciation for the opportunity cost of their own time— the benefits forgone by doing one thing instead of another.** They are also acutely aware of the ever-present assortment of obligations associated with their job—the mail that cannot be delayed, the calls that must be received, the meetings that require their participation. Managing, wrote Leonard Sayles, a Columbia University professor who studied American middle managers, is like "'keeping house' . . . where the faucets almost always drip and dust reappears as soon as it's wiped away" (1979:13).

In other words, **no matter what they are doing, managers are plagued by what they might do and what they must do.** As the head of a British football (soccer) association commented after the fans had been rioting on the continent: "In this job, one has to be permanently worried!" So managers overload themselves with work, do things abruptly, avoid wasting time. Thus, **to be superficial is an occupational hazard of managerial work.**

To succeed, managers have to become proficient at their superficiality.

It has been said that an expert is someone who knows more and more about less and less until finally he or she knows everything about nothing. The manager's problem is the opposite: knowing less and less about more and more until finally he or she knows nothing about everything. We shall return to this "Syndrome of Superficiality," as well as related conundrums, in Chapter 5.

The Action

Managers like action—activities that move, change, flow, are tangible, current, nonroutine. Don't expect most managers to spend a lot of time debating abstract issues at work; they prefer to focus on the concrete. And don't expect to find much general planning in this job, or open-ended touring; look instead for tangible delving into specific concerns. Even when it comes to scheduling, "One should never ask a busy executive to promise to do something e.g. 'next week' or even 'next Friday.' Such vague requests do not get entered into [the] appointment diary. No, one has to state a specific time, say, Friday 4:15 p.m., then it will be put down and in due course done" (Carlson 1951:71).

Managers prefer current information, often giving it top priority: interrupting meetings, rearranging agendas, and evoking flurries of activity. Of course, current information can be less reliable than that which has had a chance to settle down, get analyzed, and be compared with other information. But managers are often willing to pay this price in order to have information that is current.

If managers are so action oriented, how do they plan? Leonard Sayles offered an interesting answer:

> We . . . prefer not to consider planning and decision making as separate, distinct activities in which the manager engages. They are inextricably bound up in the warp and woof of the interaction pattern. . . . Secretary of State [John Foster] Dulles [told Dean Acheson, his predecessor, that] "he was not going to work as I had done, but would free himself from involvement with what he referred to as personnel and administrative problems, in order to have more time to think. . . . Acheson [concluded]: "This absorption with the Executive as Emerson's 'Man Thinking,' surrounded by a Cabinet of Rodin statues...seemed to me unnatural. Surely thinking is not so difficult, so hard to come by, so solemn as all this." (1964:208–209)

So the real planning of organizations takes place significantly in the heads of its managers and implicitly in the context of their daily actions, not in some abstract process reserved for a mountain retreat or in a bunch of forms to fill out. To conclude, **the pressures of managing do not encourage the development of reflective planners, the traditional literature notwithstanding. This job breeds adaptive information manipulators who prefer the live, concrete situation.**

Folklore: The manager depends on formal
information.

In keeping with the classical image of being perched on a hierarchical pedestal, managers are supposed to receive their important
information from some sort of comprehensive, formalized management information system (MIS). But this has never proved
true, not before computers, not after they appeared, not even
in these days of the Internet.

Fact: Managers tend to favor informal
communicating, especially telephone calls
and meetings, as well as e-mail.

Consider two surprising findings from earlier studies of managerial
work, the first from Carlson's study of the Swedish managing
directors:

> The only complaint heard from some of the chief executives
> [about the system of internal reports they received] was that
> the number or size of the reports had a tendency to grow
> more and more, and that it had become impossible to read
> them all. . . . These reports . . . form a part of that paper
> ballast on the executive's desk or in his briefcase, which
> is the cause of so much mental agony. (Carlson 1951:89)

This study was done just when the first computer was being
invented. Think of all the reports today! Second is this comment
from a study of MIS managers themselves:

> These managers rarely referred to computer-based infor-
> mation systems. . . . Like the shoemaker's children,

information systems managers seem to be among the last to directly benefit from the technology they purvey. (Ives and Olson 1981:57)

Soft Communication

My earlier study and others found managing to be between 60 and 90 percent oral. One CEO looked at the first piece of "hard" mail he received all week—a standard cost report—and put it aside with the comment, "I never look at this." Another CEO commented, "I don't like to write memos, as you can probably tell. I much prefer face-to-face contact."

Unlike other workers, **the manager does not leave the telephone, the meeting, or the e-mail to get back to work. These contacts *are* the work.** The manager's productive output has to be gauged largely in terms of the information he or she transmits orally or by e-mail. As Jeanne Liedtka of the Darden School has put it: **"Talk is the technology of leadership."**

As this suggests, and I found in my research, managers cherish soft information. **Gossip, hearsay, and speculation form a good part of the manager's information diet.** The reason appears to be its timeliness: today's gossip can be tomorrow's fact. The manager who is not accessible for a message advising that the firm's biggest customer was seen golfing with its main competitor may read about it as a dramatic drop in sales in next year's income statement. But by then it can be too late. To quote one manager: "I would be in trouble if the accounting reports held information I did not already have" (in Brunsson 2007:17).

Consider these words of Richard Neustadt, who studied the information-collecting habits of Presidents Roosevelt, Truman, and Eisenhower:

> It is not information of a general sort that helps a President see personal stakes; not summaries, not surveys, not the bland amalgams. Rather . . . it is the odds and ends of tangible detail that pieced together in his mind illuminate the underside of issues put before him. To help himself he must reach out as widely as he can for every scrap of fact, opinion, gossip, bearing on his interests and relationships as President. He must become his own director of his own central intelligence. (1960:153–154)

Formal information is firm, definitive, at the limit, "hard." But informal information can be much richer, even if less reliable. On the telephone, there is tone of voice and the chance to interact. In meetings, there are also facial expressions, gestures, and other body language. Never underestimate the power of these. E-mail does not offer these advantages, although it is a lot faster than conventional mail, and so somewhat more interactive.

Personal Access to the Manager

In our master's program for practicing managers (www.impm .org), the participants pair up and spend the better part of a week on "managerial exchanges" at each other's workplaces. Time and again, managers who have gone to a foreign place where they did not speak the language reported on how rich their learning was: they had to focus on these other aspects of communicating.

This raises an important concern: those people working in close proximity to their manager, because of face-to-face access, can communicate more effectively and so be better informed than others at a distance, not to mention also gain favor more easily. **We can talk all we like about a global world, but most organizations—even the most international of corporations—tend to remain rather local at their headquarters.**

Of course, managers can always get into airplanes to meet others and find out personally what is going on. But that takes time, especially compared with banging out an e-mail. So the danger may be to stay home and communicate electronically.

The Real Data Banks of the Organization

Two other concerns should be noted here as well. First, the types of information that managers favor tend to be stored in human brains. Only when written down can they be stored in electronic computers. But that takes time, and managers, as noted, are busy people. Even in e-mails, the short reply is favored over the extensive one. As a consequence, **the strategic data banks of organizations remain at least as much in the heads of their managers as in the files of their computers.**

This raises the second concern, that the nature of such information discourages the delegation of tasks. It is not as if managers can hand a dossier over to someone; they must take the time to "dump memory"—to tell that person what they know about the subject. But this could take so long that it may be easier just to do the task themselves. And so managers can be damned by their own information system to a "dilemma of delegating"—to do too much alone, or else to delegate to others without adequate briefing. We shall return to this conundrum, too, in Chapter 5.

Folklore: Managing is mostly about hierarchical relationships between "superiors" and "subordinates."

No one quite believes this statement, of course—we all know that plenty of managing happens outside and across hierarchies. But our very use of the awful labels of "superior" and "subordinate" does say something, and so, too, does our obsession with leadership, as well as our ubiquitous use of the expression "top" management, not to mention all those stuffy organizational charts.

Fact: Managing is as much about lateral relationships among colleagues and associates as it is about hierarchical relationships up and down some hierarchy.

The management literature has long slighted the importance of lateral relationships in managerial work, and it continues to do so. Yet study after study has shown that managers generally spend a great deal of their contact time—often close to half or more—with a wide variety of people external to their own units: customers, suppliers, partners, and other stakeholders, as well as all sorts of colleagues in their own organization with whom they have no direct reporting relationship.

CEOs develop extensive networks of informers, who send various reports and tell them about the latest events and opportunities. In addition, they maintain contacts with many experts (consultants, lawyers, underwriters, etc.) to provide specialized advice. And trade organization people keep them up-to-date on events in their industry.

I studied Brian Adams, program manager for a new aircraft at Bombardier, and described his job as lateral management with a vengeance. He had enormous responsibility, yet not a great deal of formal authority over many of the people he had to work with in the "partner" organizations (subcontractors, responsible for parts of the aircraft). Likewise, Charlie Zinkan, who ran the Banff National Park, sat between all sorts of interests—developers, environmentalists, and so forth—to whom he had to respond, often as delicately as possible.

We might thus characterize the manager's position as the neck of an hourglass, sitting between a network of outside contacts and the internal unit being managed. The manager receives all kinds of information and requests from insiders and outsiders, which are scanned, absorbed, and passed on to others, again both inside and outside the unit.

Folklore: Managers maintain tight control—of their time, their activities, their units.

The orchestra conductor standing on the platform waving the baton has, as noted, been a popular metaphor for managing. Here is how the first of the management gurus, Peter Drucker, put it in his classic book, *The Practice of Management:*

One analogy [for the manager] is the conductor of a symphony orchestra, through whose effort, vision and leadership, individual instrumental parts that are so much noise by them-selves, become the living whole of music. But the conductor has the composer's score: he is only the interpreter. The manager is both composer and conductor. (1954: 341–342)

Sune Carlson, who studied the working hours of nine Swedish managing directors, came up with a rather different metaphor to describe them:

Before we made the study, I always thought of a chief executive as the conductor of an orchestra, standing aloof on his platform. Now I am in some respects inclined to see him as the puppet in the puppet-show with hundreds of people pulling the strings and forcing him to act in one way or another. (1951:52)

And then came Leonard Sayles, who studied middle managers in the United States:

The manager is like a symphony orchestra conductor, endeav-oring to maintain a melodious performance in which the contributions of the various instruments are coordinated and sequenced, patterned and paced, while the orchestra members are having various personal difficulties, stage hands are moving music stands, alternating excessive heat and cold are creating audience and instrumental problems, and the sponsor of the concert is insisting on irrational changes in the program. (1964:162)

Which quote resonates with you? Managers almost always pick the third.

Fact: The manager is neither conductor nor puppet: control in this job, to the extent possible, tends to be covert more than overt, by establishing obligations to which he or she must later respond and by turning other obligations to his or her advantage.

If managerial work is like orchestra conducting, then it is not the grand image of performance, where everything has been well rehearsed and everyone is on his or her best behavior, the audience included. It is rehearsal, where all sorts of things can go wrong and must be corrected quickly.

The truth, however, is that effective managers appear to be neither conductors nor puppets: they exercise control despite the constraints by making use of two degrees of freedom in particular. They make a set of initial decisions that define many of their subsequent commitments (e.g., start a project that, once underway, demands their time). And they adapt to their own ends activities in which they must engage (e.g., by using a ceremonial occasion to lobby for their organization).

In other words, **successful managers create some of their own obligations and take advantage of others. Their success comes not necessarily from having the greatest degrees of freedom but by using to advantage whatever degrees of freedom they can create.** Put differently, all managers appear to be puppets: some decide who will pull the strings, and how, while others get overwhelmed by this demanding job.

THE IMPACT OF THE INTERNET

There has been one evident change in recent times that should be having a great effect on all these characteristics of managing: the Internet, especially e-mail, a medium of communication that has dramatically increased speed and volume in the transmission of information. Has its impact on managing been likewise dramatic?

Judging by all the e-mails flying about and the ubiquitousness of mobile devices, it would certainly seem so. But the question is whether this has changed managing fundamentally. The studies are few, but the answer appears to be yes and no.

No, because the Internet may be mostly reinforcing the very characteristics that have long been prevalent in managerial work, as discussed in this chapter. And yes, because this may be driving some of the practice of managing over the edge.

Better-informed managers, able to communicate more quickly, may develop faster-moving, more competitive organizations. But some managers may be drawn into acting less thoughtfully, by conforming more and considering less.

The Media and Its Message

It is important to note, for starters, that this new medium remains thin. **Like conventional mail, e-mail is restricted by the poverty of words alone.** There is no tone of voice to hear, no gestures to see, no presence to feel. (Does ☺ or "LOL" do it for you?) Managing is as much about all these things as it is about the factual content of the messages.

While giving the impression of being "in touch," the only thing actually being touched is a keyboard. This can aggravate a long-standing problem in managing: allowing a fancy new technology to give the illusion of control.

On the telephone, people can interrupt, grunt, argue, truly laugh out loud; in meetings, they can nod in agreement or nod off in boredom. Effective managers pick up on such clues. With e-mail, you don't quite know how someone has reacted until the reply comes back, and even then you cannot be sure if the words were carefully chosen or sent in haste.

Marshall McLuhan (1962) wrote famously about the "global village" created by new information technologies. But what kind of a village is that?

In the traditional village, you chat with your neighbors at the local market: this is the heart of the community. In the global village, you click to send a message to someone on the other side of the globe, who you may never even have met. Like those fantasy-ridden love affairs on the Internet, such relationships can remain untouched and untouchable.

Organizations are communities, dependent on the robustness of their relationships. Trust and respect are absolutely key. So we have to be quite careful about this global village, not to confuse its networks with communities. **The Internet may be enhancing networks while weakening communities, within organizations and across them.**

Effects of E-mail on Managing

One thing is certain: e-mail increases the pace and pressures of managing, and likely the interruptions as well. A laptop on the table is one thing, an iPhone in the pocket quite another: the tether to the global village. As for the orientation to action, the irony is that e-mail, technically removed from the action, enhances the action-orientation of managing: do it fast, reply NOW!

E-mail helps to extend the manager's contacts; everyone becomes within easy reach. But this may come at the expense of deeper communication—say, with the colleagues down the hall. **Is all that global networking coming at the expense of local conversing?**

As with most technologies, the Internet can be used for better and for worse. You can be mesmerized by it, and so let it manage you. Or you can understand its powers as well as its dangers, and so manage it. I have written this section of the book to encourage the latter—namely, to discourage ostensible conductors from becoming puppets.

The conclusion reached in a paper I did with our dean, an IT specialist (Mintzberg and Todd 2012), is that **the Internet is not changing the practice of management fundamentally; rather, it is reinforcing characteristics that we have been seeing for decades.** But the devil can be in the detail. **The Internet may be driving much management practice over the edge, making it so frenetic that it becomes dysfunctional: too superficial, too disconnected, too conformist.**

NORMALLY CALCULATED CHAOS

To conclude, this chapter has presented the characteristics of managing, as they were earlier and remain now. Do these suggest bad managing? Not at all. They suggest normal managing. But they are acceptable only within limits. Exceed them, and the practice of management can become dysfunctional. We all know frenetic managers who have lost it. What seemed normal one day became hazardous the next.

Managing, even normal managing, is no easy job. A *New York Times* commentary on my original study (Andrews 1976) used two phrases that capture the nature of this well: "calculated chaos" and "controlled disorder." They tell of the nuance that effective managing requires—compared with the "confusing chaos" of "naïve managers" (Sayles 1979:19). With this in mind, let's turn to the content of managing—what managers actually do—and return to how managers can deal with these pressures in Chapter 5.

3 Managing Information, People, Action

A model of managing

We begin this discussion of what managers actually do with the gurus of management, most of whom have seen this job in its component parts, not as an integrated whole. This chapter proposes a model of managing that positions the parts within the whole, by depicting **managing as taking place on three planes: through information, with people, and for action.** A final section describes the "well-rounded" job of managing.

MANAGING ONE ROLE AT A TIME

If you wish to become one of those "gurus" of management, focus on one aspect of the job to the exclusion of all the others. Henri Fayol saw managing as controlling, while Tom Peters has seen it as doing? ("'Don't think, do' is the phrase I favor'" [1990]). On Wall Street, of course, managers "do deals." Michael Porter has instead equated managing with thinking, specifically analyzing ("I favor a set of analytical techniques for developing strategy," he wrote in *The Economist* [1987:2]). Others, such as Warren Bennis, have built their reputations among managers by describing their work as leading, while Herbert Simon built his among academics by describing it as decision making. (The *Harvard Business Review* concurred, for years pronouncing on its cover, "The magazine of decision makers.")

Each of them is wrong because all of them are right. Managing is not one of these things but all of them: it is controlling and doing and dealing and thinking and leading and deciding and more, not added up but blended together. Take away any one of these , and you do not have the full job of managing. By focusing on one aspect of the job to the exclusion of the others, each of these gurus has narrowed our perception of managing rather than broadening it.

Go beyond the gurus, to some of the less popular fare of the academics, and you find a kind of acknowledgment of this problem: they offer many lists of managerial roles. The good news is that these are more comprehensive; the bad news is that they take the job apart without putting it back together. Managing thus looks like Humpty Dumpty, lying in broken pieces on the ground.

Some years ago, I set out to bond all these pieces into a cohesive model. The idea was to get it all on to one diagram, so that the reader could consider all the aspects of managing together— comprehensively. The result is shown in Figure 3. (If it looks like an egg, consider it as Humpty Dumpty back together again.)

The first time I showed this diagram to a manager—a friend, over dinner, working in a film company—he immediately pointed to where he saw the strengths and the weaknesses of the managers

FIGURE 3 **A Model of Managing**

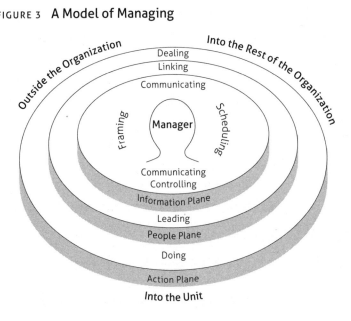

with whom he worked. Another manager, with the World Health Organization, wrote to me that "I could instantly see the roles from which I tend to shy away or not do so well. In that sense, [the model] challenged me more."

AN OVERVIEW OF THE MODEL

The model shows the manager between the unit he or she manages (inside) and the world outside it—the rest of the organization (unless the manager is chief executive of the entire organization) as well as what is around the organization (customers, trade officials, etc.).

The overriding purpose of managing is to ensure that the unit serves *its* basic purpose, whether to sell products in a retail chain or care for the elderly in a nursing home. This requires the taking of *actions*, which managers sometimes do themselves. More commonly, however, they take one or two steps back from the action. One step back, they encourage other *people* to take action—by coaching, motivating, building teams, strengthening culture, and so forth. Two steps back, they use *information* to guide other people to take action: imposing a target on a sales team, sharing information about a customer, and so forth.

On the day she was observed, Carol Haslam, head of Hawsk-head Films, could be seen working on all three planes. On the action plane, she was deeply involved with developing projects for new films—she was doing deals galore. On the people plane, she was maintaining her vast network of contacts used to promote these projects, as well as building teams of filmmakers to execute them. And on the information plane, all day long she was collecting and disseminating ideas, data, advice, and other information.

Two roles are shown on each plane. On the information plane, managers *communicate* (all around) and *control* (inside). On the people plane, they *lead* (inside) and *link* (to the outside). And on the action plane, they *do* (inside) and *deal* (outside). Also shown, managers *frame* (conceive strategies, establish priorities, etc.) and *schedule* (their own time). Each aspect of the model is discussed in turn before all are discussed together in conclusion.

FRAMING AND SCHEDULING

Framing defines how a manager identifies purpose, by focusing on issues and developing strategies. **Framing establishes the context for everyone else working in the unit.** Alain Noël (1989) has referred to this as the managers' *preoccupations,* as compared with their *occupations* (what they actually do)—which can sometimes amount to a single "magnificent obsession."

Brian Adams, program manager for the Global Express aircraft at Bombardier, had a magnificent obsession, imposed by the senior management: to "get it in the air" by June. "Then, we'll see," he commented. In contrast, John Cleghorn, CEO of the Royal Bank of Canada, had a variety of preoccupations as its chairman, concerning the improvement and success of the company.

Scheduling is of central concern to all managers: their agenda inevitably gets a lot of attention. More than a half century ago, Sune Carlson noted how managers "become slaves to their appointment diaries—they get a kind of 'diary complex'" (1951:71). **Scheduling brings the frame to life, by determining what the manager seeks to do and how to use his or her available degrees of freedom to do it.**

Moreover, the manager's schedule can have enormous influence over everyone else in the unit: **Whatever gets into the manager's agenda is taken as a signal of what matters in the unit.** In fact, when managers schedule, they are often allocating not only their own time but also that of the people who report to them.

Scheduling amounts to what Peters and Waterman (1982) have called "chunking"—slicing up managerial concerns into distinct tasks, to be carried out in specific slots of time. The problem, of course (which we shall discuss in Chapter 5), is how to put back together that which has been taken apart. And this is where the frame comes in: if clear, it can function as a magnet to draw the distinct chunks into a coherent whole.

MANAGING THROUGH INFORMATION

To manage through information means to sit two steps removed from the ultimate purpose of managing: information is processed by the manager to guide other people to take the necessary actions. In other words, on this plane the manager focuses neither on people nor on actions directly, but on information as an indirect way to make things happen.

While this was the classic view of managing, which dominated perceptions of its practice for much of the last century, it has again become prevalent, thanks to current obsessions with the **"bottom line" and "shareholder value": both encourage a detached, essentially information-driven practice of managing.**

Two main roles describe managing on the information plane, one labeled *communicating,* to promote the flow of information all around the manager, and the other labeled *controlling,* to drive behavior in the unit.

Communicating All Around the Unit

Watch any manager and one thing readily becomes apparent: the great amount of time spent simply *communicating—* namely, collecting and disseminating information for its own

sake, without necessarily processing it. Studies indicate that managers often spend about half their time doing this.

> *Norm Inkster, head of the RCMP, went over press clippings of the past twenty-four hours; John Cleghorn briefed institutional investors on happenings at the bank; Stephen Omollo, manager of a Red Cross refugee camp in Tanzania, inspected the reconstruction of a fence that had been blown over in a storm.*

The communicating role is a kind of membrane all around the manager, through which all activities pass. There are four aspects to this:

The Manager Is Monitor. Managers reach out for every scrap of useful information they can get—about internal operations and external events, trends and analyses, everything imaginable. They are also bombarded with such information, much of it as a consequence of the networks they build up for themselves. Thus, Morris et al. wrote about high school principals touring the halls, visiting the cafeteria, making quick checks in the classrooms and libraries, and more—a "constant bobbing" in and out, in order to "gauge the school climate" and "anticipate and quell potential trouble" (1981:74).

As a Result, the Manager Is the Nerve Center of the Unit. The manager is the relative generalist in the unit, overseeing the more specialized jobs. He or she may not know that much about any particular specialty but is in a position to know something about all of them. Thus, **the manager becomes the *nerve center* of the unit—its best-informed member.** As Morris et al. put it:

"the principal is . . . the information switchboard through which all important messages pass" (1982:690).

The same holds true for external information. By virtue of his or her status, the manager has access to outside managers who are themselves nerve centers of their own units. Just as one factory foreman can call another factory foreman, so too can the president of the United States call the prime minister of Great Britain. Consider this description of one of those presidents:

> The essence of Roosevelt's technique for information-gathering was competition. "He would call you in," one of his aides once told me, "and he'd ask you to get the story on some complicated business, and you'd come back after a couple of days of hard labor and present the juicy morsel you'd uncovered under a stone somewhere, and *then* you'd find out he knew all about it, along with something else you *didn't* know." (Neustadt 1960:157)

The Manager Is Disseminator. Much of the manager's information is simply disseminated to other people in the unit. **Like bees, managers cross-pollinate.** Allen Burchill, commanding officer of the RCMP in the province of Nova Scotia, commented on his way to a management meeting with his reports, "I'm informed. But this is a go-around to make sure they're informed."

The Manager Is Spokesperson. The manager also sends much of the information out—for example, to customers, suppliers, and government officials. **As spokesperson for the unit, the manager represents it to the outside world, speaking to various publics on its behalf, lobbying for its causes, representing its**

expertise in public forums, and keeping outside stakeholders up-to-date on its progress.

The Verbal, the Visual, and the Visceral. It should be evident now that the manager's advantage lies not in documented information, which can be made available to anyone, but in current information transmitted largely by word of mouth—for example, the gossip, hearsay, and opinion discussed in the last chapter. Indeed, much of an informed manager's information is not even verbal so much as visual and visceral—in other words, seen and felt more than heard.

To conclude discussion of the communicating role, **the job of managing is significantly one of information processing, especially through a great deal of listening, seeing, and feeling, besides just talking.** But this can damn a manager to a job of overwork or one of frustration. On one side, there is the temptation to get in there and find out personally what is going on—to "avoid the sterility so often found in those who isolate themselves from operations" (Wrapp 1967:92). The danger, of course, is micromanaging: meddling in the work of others. But on the other side is "macroleading": simply not knowing what's going on. We shall return to this in Chapter 5.

Controlling Inside the Unit

One direct use of the manager's information is to "control"—that is, to direct the behavior of "subordinates." As noted earlier, for the better part of the last century, managing was considered almost synonymous with controlling. It is more than that, but control of the unit through the exercise of formal authority remains one important part of the job.

> *In managing the refugee camps in Tanzania, controlling was front and center, simply because so much that happened had to be kept under tight wraps, for fear of a small incident blowing into a major crisis. "You just need to put your ear to the ground, Stephen, and find out more about what the feelings are among the refugees," Abbas Gullet, head of the delegation, told Stephen Omollo, in charge of the camps themselves, so that he could get in there and stop any impending problem. On top of this were the many Red Cross systems, procedures, rules, and regulations. In contrast, the day with orchestra conductor Bramwell Tovey exhibited much less overt controlling. He hardly "directed" on this day, in the sense of giving orders, delegating tasks, and authorizing decisions.*

The *Oxford English Dictionary* traces the word *manager* to the French—specifically, the word *main*, meaning "hand," in reference to "the training, handling, and directing of a horse in its paces." In management, this means to ensure that people accomplish their work. **Controlling has to be done, but the trick is to avoid being captured by it, so that it comes to dominate the work of managing.**

Decision making is considered to be a thinking process in the mind of the decider, to make choices. But there is more to decision making than that. In fact, we can understand decision making more fully by seeing it as various forms of controlling:

Decision Making as Designing. Managers design things—projects, structures, systems— in order to guide the behavior of their reports. Robert Simons (1995) of the Harvard Business School found in his research that corporate chief executives tend to select one system (e.g., profit planning) and make it key to their exercise of control.

Decision Making as Delegating. Here the manager identifies the need to get something done but delegates the specific deciding and the doing to someone else in the unit.

Decision Making as Authorizing. In this case, decision making reduces to passing judgment on the decisions of others. Consider this comment by Andy Grove, as chief executive of Intel:

> To be sure, once in a while we managers in fact *make* a decision. But for every time that happens, we *participate* in the making of many, many others, and we do that in a variety of ways. We provide factual inputs or just offer opinions, we debate the pros and cons of alternatives and thereby force a better decision to emerge, we review decisions made or about to be made by others, encourage or discourage them, ratify or veto them. (1983:50–51)

Decision Making as Allocating Resources. Managers devote a good deal of their decision making, including within their budgeting systems, to the allocation of resources—money, materials, and equipment, as well as the efforts of other people. They also do this by scheduling their own time and designing the organization structures that influence how other people in their unit allocate their time.

Note that to treat something as a "resource" is to consider it as information, for the purpose of control. So to "allocate resources" is to function on the information plane of managing, in the role of controlling. Indeed, **treating employees as "human resources" means to deal with them as if they are just information: they get reduced to a narrow dimension of their whole selves.**

Decision Making as Deeming. Finally, there is deeming, which has become an increasingly popular form of controlling, but hardly under that label. ("Management by objectives" is a better-known one.) By deeming, I mean imposing targets on people: "Increase sales by 10 percent," or "Reduce costs by 20 percent." All too often these days, when managers don't know what to do, they drive their reports to "perform." And this includes a good deal of so-called strategic planning, which often reduces the strategy process to an exercise in "number crunching." "Increase sales by 10 percent" is not a strategy. (More on this later; see also Mintzberg [1994c and 1994d].)

Managers have to get beyond the targets—into the workings of their units. Put differently, **some deeming is fine; management by deeming is not.** Every manager certainly has to manage on the information plane; but none can stop there, by failing to manage on the people and the action planes.

MANAGING WITH PEOPLE

To manage *with* people, instead of *through* information, is to move one step closer to action but still to remain removed from it. On this plane, the manager helps other people make things happen: *they* are the doers.

Managing on the people plane requires a wholly different attitude from managing on the information plane. There the manager guides people to specific ends. Here people are not guided so much as encouraged, often to ends they favor naturally.

These comments apply to managing inside the unit, with people who report formally to its manager. But, as noted in the last chapter, managers generally spend at least as much time with people outside their units. On the people plane, therefore, we discuss two managerial roles: *leading* people inside the unit and *linking* to people outside it.

Leading People Inside the Unit

When a specialist becomes a manager, the biggest shift has to be from "I" to "we." The first instinct may be "Good, now I can make the decisions and issue the orders." Soon, however, comes the realization that "formal authority is a very limited source of power," that to become a manager is to become "more dependent . . . on others to get things done" (Hill 2003:262). Enter the role of *leading*.

More has been written about leadership than probably all other aspects of managing combined. Find an organization with a problem and you will find all kinds of people proposing leadership as the solution. And if a new leader comes in and things do improve, no matter why (a stronger economy, a bankrupt competitor), they will have been proven right. This is part of our "Romance of Leadership" (Meindl et al. 1985).

The leading role can certainly make a difference. But it is no more the be-all and end-all of managing than is controlling or decision making. In fact, I believe **we need to see leadership as a necessary component of management.**

Managers exercise such leadership in three ways: with *individuals* (one-on-one), with *teams,* and with the *whole unit or organization* (in terms of its culture).[1]

Leading Means Helping to Energize Individuals. Managers spend a good deal of time persuading people, supporting them, convincing them, encouraging them. Perhaps this is best put another way: **In the leading role, managers help to bring out the energy that exists naturally within people.** To quote the words of one CEO: "It's not [the manager's] job to supervise or to motivate, but to liberate and enable" (Max DePree of Herman Miller, 1990).

So be careful of some of the popular leadership terms here. For example, *participation* and *empowerment* keep people subordinate, because these come at the behest of the manager. Truly empowered people, such as doctors in a hospital, even bees in a hive, do not await gifts from their managerial gods; they know what they are there to do and just do it. In fact, a good deal of what is today called "empowerment" is really just getting rid of years of disempowerment. **Empowerment is what managers do *to* people. Engagement is what managers do *with* people.**

---

[1]A third set of related managerial activities—including hiring, judging, remunerating, promoting, and dismissing individuals—falls under the role of controlling, not leading, because these are about making decisions. Of course, *how* a manager carries out these activities can put him or her on the people plane. But that is true of every managerial role, doing and dealing no less than controlling and communicating.

Leading Means Helping to Develop Individuals. Managers also coach, train, mentor, teach, counsel, nurture, in general help develop the individuals in their unit. Again, this vast array of labels indicates just how much attention this aspect of leading has received. But **the responsibility for development is perhaps best seen as managers helping people to develop themselves** (see www.CoachingOurselves.com). Two schoolteachers in Calgary take this further, in the context of the classroom: "We lose patience with the idea that the teacher is there mainly to 'facilitate' children's development. . . . We are there for something more subtle and profound than that: we help mediate the knowledge, problems and questions the children already possess" (Clifford and Friesen 1993:19).

Leading Means Helping to Build and Maintain Teams. On the group level, managers play key roles in building and maintaining teams inside their own units. **Team building involves bonding people into cooperative groups as well as resolving conflicts within and between these groups so that they can get on with their work.** For example, successful athletics teams have an "almost uncanny ability to perform as a single unit, with the efforts of individual members blending seamlessly together." Management as "a team sport . . . makes similar demands on its players" (Kraut et al. 2005:122).

The new managers Hill studied initially conceived of their "people-management role as building the most effective relationships they [could] with each *individual* subordinate," and so they "fail[ed] to recognize, much less address, their team-building responsibilities." But over time, after mistakes, they realized the importance of this (2003:284).

Perhaps "new managers get fooled" by organizational structure: "they assume that if all workers do their jobs according to some master plan or direction, there will be no need for contact or human intervention" (Sayles 1979:22). In other words, the controlling role will take care of the necessary coordination. It rarely does.

Leading Means Helping to Establish and Strengthen Culture. Finally, in the full unit, and more commonly for the chief executive of an entire organization, managers play a key role in establishing and strengthening the culture.

Culture is intended to do collectively what other aspects of the leading role do for individuals and groups: encourage the best efforts of people, by aligning their interests with the needs of the organization. **In contrast to decision *making* as a form of controlling, culture is decision *shaping* as a form of leading.** As Mary Parker Follett put it in 1920: "We need leaders, not masters or drivers. . . . This is the power which creates community" (p. 230). "[A]nd so, one principal roam[ed] the school reminding teachers and students of their duties and exhorting all participants in the learning process to strive for good work and exemplary performance" (Morris et al. 1982:691).

Here, beyond being the nerve center of the unit's information, **the manager can be described as the energy center of the unit's culture.** As William F. Whyte put it in a classic study of street gangs:

> The leader is the focal point for the organization of his group. In his absence, the members of the gang are divided into a number of small groups. There is no common activity or general conversation. When the leader appears, the situation

changes strikingly. The small units form into one large group. The conversation becomes general, and unified action frequently follows. (1955:258)

Consider the queen bee in the hive: "She issues no orders; she obeys, as meekly as the humblest of her subjects. This we will term the 'spirit of the hive'" (Maeterlinck 1901). But by her very presence, manifested in the emitting of a chemical substance, she unites the members of the hive and galvanizes them into action. In human organizations, we call this substance **culture: it is the spirit of the human hive.**

The culture of an organization may be difficult to establish, and to improve—that can take years, if ever—but it can easily be destroyed, given a neglectful management. That is why the sustaining of culture was front and center on several of the days I spent with managers of long-established organizations:

In a police force, we might expect to see a good deal of conventional controlling, in the form of rules, performance standards, and forms to fill out. There was no shortage of that on the days I spent with three RCMP managers. But greater emphasis seemed to be put on culture: controlling behavior through the sharing of norms, based on careful socialization. For example, Commissioner Inkster visited the officer training school and spoke extemporaneously for a half hour, followed by a blunt period of questions and answers.

To conclude this discussion of the role of leading, we can return to the metaphor of the leader as conductor on the platform, fully in control. Does that actually constitute the exercise of leadership? See the accompanying box.

◼ MYTHS OF THE ORCHESTRA CONDUCTOR AS LEADER

In the metaphor of the manager as orchestra conductor, we have leadership captured perfectly in caricature. The great chief stands on the podium, with the followers arranged neatly around, ready to respond to every command. The maestro raises the baton, and they all play in perfect unison. Another motion and they all stop. Absolutely in charge—a manager's dream: a signal to sales, another to marketing, and they play in perfect harmony. The perfect myth!

As Bramwell Tovey, conductor of the Winnipeg Symphony, was quick to point out, this is an organization of subordination, and that includes the conductor. Mozart pulls the strings. How else to explain the phenomenon of "guest conductor"? Try to imagine a "guest manager" in almost any other kind of organization.

In fact, these "conductors" and "directors" engage in orchestra *operating* more than orchestra *leading*. Rehearsals, as noted, are key—that is when the real managing takes place. A concert is, in effect, a project, and project management happens in rehearsals, when pace, pattern, tempo, and sound are perfected.

When asked about his leadership, Bramwell replied, "We never talk about 'the relationship,'" which he called "covert leadership." Yet leadership was clearly on his mind. He told me that he was not allowed to single out individuals in rehearsals and said in jest, "I don't see my job as a manager. I look on it more as a lion tamer!" It's a good line, but it hardly captures the image of seventy tame pussycats sitting in neatly ordered rows ready to play together at the flick of a wand.

And what does culture building mean here? Seventy people come together for rehearsals and then disperse. When is the culture built? Perhaps also covertly, through the energy, attitude, and general behavior of the conductor. But beyond this, culture is built into the very system: this was not just the culture of the Winnipeg Symphony Orchestra, but of symphony orchestras in general, which had been developing for centuries.

So beware, all you fans of leadership. One day you may wake up to find that Bramwell Tovey is what a good deal of contemporary managing is all about. Then you will have to step off your hierarchical podiums, lay down your budgetary batons, and get down on the ground, where the real work of your organization takes place—where you and your colleagues can make beautiful music together. (Adapted from Mintzberg 1998.)

Linking to People Outside the Unit

Still on the people plane, **linking looks out the way leading looks in. The focus is on the web of relationships that managers maintain with numerous individuals and groups outside their units.** "When compared to non-managers, managers show wider organizational membership networks—they belong to more clubs, societies, and the like" (Carroll and Teo 1996:437). But each manager does this in his or her own way.

The three managers I observed in the Canadian parks all managed on the edges—between their units and the outside context—but in each case a different one. Sandy Davis, head of the Western Region, managed especially on a political edge, between her parks and the officials in Ottawa. She connected politics to process. Charlie Zinkan, head of the Banff National Park, who reported to Sandy, managed especially on a stakeholder edge, as various outsiders brought pressures to bear on him. He connected influence to programs. And Gord Irwin, Front Country Manager in the Banff National Park, who reported to Charlie, functioned especially on an operating edge, between the operations and the administration. He connected administration to action.

It is surprising how little attention linking has received in the writings on management, despite the evidence from study after study that **managers are external linkers as much as they are internal leaders.** This is hardly understandable, especially now, given the prevalence of alliances, joint ventures, and other collaborative relationships.

Managers link with customers, suppliers, partners, public officials, union organizers, and many others, as well as with line and staff people in their own organizations. One school principal even "cultivate[d] . . . grandmothers"—neighborhood residents who knew the community well and so could act as "spotters" for the school, "warn[ing] him of unusual developments" (Morris et al. 1982:689).

Fabienne Lavoie on the hospital ward connected to doctors, patients, and families of patients. John Cleghorn lunched with financial investors of the Royal Bank, informing them in order to influence them, while Brian Adams worked with partner companies of Bombardier from all over the world.

A model of the manager's linking role is shown in Figure 4, the components of which are discussed in turn.

Linking Means Networking. One thing is clear. **Networking is pervasive: almost all managers spend a good deal of time building up networks of outside contacts and establishing coalitions of external supporters.**

FIGURE 4   **A Model of Linking**

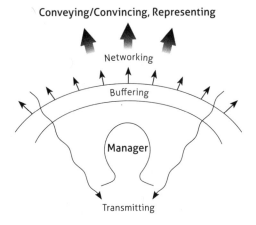

Conveying/Convincing, Representing

Networking

Buffering

Manager

Transmitting

Carol Haslam, managing director at Hawkshead Films, brokered between clients and producers, drawing on what seemed to be an immense web of contacts and a finely tuned understanding of the British television industry. In the Red Cross refugee camps, Abbas Gullet exhibited a particular ability to bridge, not only between English and Swahili as well as Africans and Europeans, but also between a head office in a wealthy European city and its local office in an impoverished African township.

Linking Means Representing. Looking out, **managers play a *figurehead* role, representing their units officially to the outside world**, whether it be a company CEO presiding at some formal dinner, a university dean signing diplomas for graduating students, or a factory foreman greeting visiting customers. (Someone once said, only half in jest, that the manager is the person who meets the visitors so that everyone else can get their work done.)

Bramwell Tovey spent an evening at the home of the most generous supporter of the orchestra, who was hosting "The Maestro's Circle." There he socialized with about fifty of the orchestra's supporters, gave a short speech, and then entertained them on the piano.

Linking Means Conveying and Convincing. Managers use their networks to gain support for their units. This may entail (on the information plane) simply *conveying* information to appropriate outsiders—for example, telling those grandmothers in the vicinity of the school to watch out for drug dealers. Or it may be done (on the people plane) to **champion the needs of the unit, *lobby* for its causes, *promote* its products, and just plain *peddle influence for it.***

A good part of the day that I observed Rony Brauman, head of Doctors Without Borders, he was giving press and media interviews, representing the views of the organization on the situation in Somalia, to influence public opinion. He was "speaking out" more than just speaking.

Linking Means Transmitting. Linking is a two-way street: **Managers who peddle influence out are the targets of ped-dled influence coming in, a good deal of which has to be *transmitted* to others in the unit.**

For Brian Adams of Bombardier to get that new airplane in the air on time, everything had to come together on a tight schedule. So he had to transmit to his engineers the pressures that came to him from suppliers and his own senior management. Likewise, Carol Haslam of Hawskhead had to ensure that the internal making of the films was responsive to the external concerns of the clients.

Linking Means Buffering. It is in the combination of all these linking activities that we can especially appreciate the delicate balancing acts of managing. Managers are not just *channels* through which pass information and influence. They are also *valves* in these channels, who control what gets passed on, and how. To use two other popular words, **managers are *gatekeepers and buffers* in the flow of influence.** To appreciate the importance of this, consider five ways by which managers can get it wrong:

- Some managers are *sieves* who let influence flow too easily into their unit. This can drive their reports crazy, forcing them to respond to every pressure, as when, for example, corporate chief executives transmit the demands of stock market analysts into pressures on every employee to drive up short-term results.
- Other managers are *dams* who block out too much of the external influence—for example, from customers asking for product changes. This may protect the people inside the unit, but it detaches them from the outside world.
- Then there are the *sponges*—managers who absorb most of the pressures themselves. This may be appreciated by others, but it is only a matter of time before these managers burn themselves out.
- Managers acting as *hoses* turn the pressures on the people outside, who may as a consequence become angry and less

inclined to cooperate. This is common when a company squeezes its suppliers excessively.

■ Finally, there are the *drips*, who exert too little pressure on the people outside, so that the needs of the unit are not well represented. Examples are CEOs who don't push back to those stock market analysts at the expense of the health of their companies.

The effective manager may act in each of these ways some of the time but does not allow any of them to dominate all of the time. In other words, **managing on the edges—the boundaries between the unit and its context—is a tricky business: every unit has to be protected, responsive, and aggressive, depending on the circumstances.**

MANAGING ACTION

If managers manage through information—conceptually, from a distance—and with people—closer, with affect—then on this third plane they manage action directly—actively, concretely—as when someone comments, "Mary-Anne is a doer." Yet how often do we read about managing as doing, compared with managing as leading or as decision making?

Linda Hill's new managers recognized this only after they were well into their jobs. "When asked at the end of the first months, what is a manager, the new managers no longer responded 'being the boss' or 'being the person in control.' Instead, the most common observations included being a 'trouble-shooter,' a 'juggler,' and a 'quick-change artist'" (2003:57).

Catherine Joint-Dieterle, head of the fashion museum in Paris,
played a major role in the bringing in of new garments and
reviewing each as it arrived. She was personally involved in
the public tours of the museum. She wrote the proposals for
new exhibitions.

In the vernacular, managers "champion change," "manage projects," "fight fires," "do deals." Some of this pertains to actions taken within the unit, discussed here as *doing on the inside*; while others happen beyond the unit, discussed as *dealing on the outside.*

Doing on the Inside

What does it mean for a manager to be a doer? Many managers, after all, hardly "do" anything. Some don't even place their own telephone calls. Watch a manager at work and what you see is a lot of talking and listening, not doing.

Doing in the context of managing usually means *almost* doing— that is, getting close to the taking of action: managing it directly, rather than indirectly with people or through information. So **the manager as "doer" is really the person who "gets it done,"** as in the French expression *faire faire* (literally, "to make something get made").

What is it that managers actually do? This relates to what the unit gets done, the actions that it takes—whether to produce a product in a company or deliver a baby in a hospital. The manager's involvement is not passive: this is not about sitting in an office and giving orders. Deeming is not doing. Nor is designing strategies, structures, and systems to drive other people. All of that is controlling. In the doing role, the manager gets personally involved in the actions, "hands-on," that determine what the unit gets done.

Some years ago, when the time came to redesign Pampers, Proctor & Gamble's most important product, the chief executive of the whole company headed up the task force. When Johnson & Johnson faced a crisis after someone tampered with a few of its Tylenol packages, it was the CEO who headed up the response effort (Bennis 1989). These examples suggest that **there are two aspects of the doing role: managing projects proactively and handling disturbances reactively.**

Doing Means Engaging in Projects. Managers can choose to head up projects themselves, or join others on them, for a variety of reasons. Sometimes it is to *learn,* or to *inform* themselves about something they need to know (on the information plane). Other times it is to *demonstrate*—that is, encourage others to take action, or show them how to do so (on the people plane). But most commonly, perhaps, managers involve themselves in projects because they are concerned about the *outcomes* (on the action plane).

Jacques Benz, director-general of GSI, was an active participant in a meeting about a software platform being developed for the French Post Office. After listening for some time, he commented, "There's a choice to make"; later he gave some advice; and at the end of the meeting, he pushed for what was needed at the next meeting. Asked why he attended, Jacques replied that the project was setting a precedent for the company, "the beginning of a strategy."

Of course, few managers can take personal charge of all their unit's projects. But **the suggestion in some of the literature that managers should "do" nothing—doing being dismissed as micromanaging—stems from a sterile view of the job: the manager on a pedestal, out of literal "touch," simply pronouncing strategies for everyone else to implement.** As reported by an executive in the motorcycle business: "The Chief Executive of a world famous group of management consultants tried hard to convince me that it is ideal that top level management executives should have as little knowledge as possible relative to the product. This great man really believed that this qualification enabled them to deal efficiently with all business matters in a detached and uninhibited way" (Hopwood 1981:173).

This might work fine in a simple world. Ours, unfortunately, is a messy one. So managers have to find out what's going on. And one sensible way is to get involved in specific projects. **Strategies are not immaculately conceived in detached offices. They are learned through tangible experiences** (more on this in Chapter 5). Put differently, projects don't just execute strategies; they help to establish them in the first place, as Jacques Benz suggested. Managers *off* the ground tend not to learn—and thus often turn out to be failed strategists.

With all sorts of other responsibilities, managers cannot usually allow themselves to focus on one project—that "magnificent obsession" mentioned earlier. But there can be important exceptions—for example, when the unit is in crisis or is facing a magnificent opportunity. Plus there are project managers, such as Brian Adams at Bombardier, whose job focus is on one project.

For most managers, however, a variety of projects demands attention. Since these tend to proceed irregularly, with many delays, the manager can work on each intermittently, occasionally giving it a boost and then turning to other concerns.

Doing Means Handling Disturbances. If managing projects is largely about proactive change in the unit—pursuing opportunities—then handling disturbances is about reacting to changes forced on the unit. An unforeseen event, a problem long ignored, the appearance of a new competitor may precipitate a disturbance, and a correction becomes necessary.

The day I observed Alan Whelan at BT was largely about a major disturbance—the failure to get sign-off from the senior management on a large contract. At Bombardier, Brian Adams had to intervene with a "problem supplier" of the airplane. And at the hospital in the refugee camp, Abbas Gullet faced a crisis, due to the inadvertent firing of its head nurse.

As managers advance to senior positions, they "deal increasingly with predicaments, not problems." These "require interpretative thinking;" they "cannot be handled smoothly" (Farson 1996:43).

Why must the manager be the one to respond? Aren't others in the unit there to do that? Sure, and often they do. But some disturbances require the manager's formal authority or their nerve center information. And others concern issues that no one else can appreciate—for example, the reaction of a key stakeholder. Moreover, problems often degenerate into disturbances precisely because they have fallen between the cracks: no one in the unit has taken responsibility, so the manager has to do so. Or a disturbance arises that no one else can handle better than the manager. Returning to that Johnson & Johnson story, in the words of the company's chief executive who "took charge immediately" after poison was found in some of its Tylenol capsules:

> I knew I had to and I knew I could. . . . I knew the media. I was a news freak, and I'd dealt with the networks several times. I knew the heads of news, who to call, how to talk with them. . . . I was in this room twelve hours a day. I solicited advice from everyone, because no one had ever dealt with this kind of issue before. . . . We put together the new packaging overnight practically, when it would have normally taken two years. (in Bennis 1989:152–154)

There is no shortage of reported stories about disturbances that arose because of incompetent or at least neglectful management. Fair enough, much of the time. Less discussed, but equally worth noting, are disturbances that occur naturally in every organization (as in the Tylenol example). In fact, **the effective organization may be, not just the one that avoids many disturbances, but also the one that deals effectively with the unexpected disturbances that do arise.** Indeed, the more innovative the organization, the more likely are disturbances to arise unexpectedly. The organization that doesn't take risks may avoid all disturbances until the one that sinks it in the end.

One other aspect of disturbance handling merits mention here. Sometimes a manager substitutes for someone in the unit who is ill, has quit unexpectedly, or otherwise cannot do the job. Here the manager engages in the regular work of the unit. But since he or she is disturbance handling—filling in by exception—this should be considered part of the job of managing.

There are times, of course, when managers simply choose to do some of the regular operating work of their organization: the pope leads prayers, a hospital chief does clinical work on Fridays. Perhaps they simply enjoy this work and would otherwise miss it, in which case it is no more managing than is a weekly game of tennis (at least without a client). But there may be managerial reasons behind these activities, too: the pope may be acting as figurehead, and the hospital chief may be keeping in touch.

To conclude discussion of the doing role, Chester Barnard, CEO of New Jersey Bell years ago, wrote that "executive work is not that of the organization, but the specialized work of *maintaining* the organization in operation" (1938:215). It sounds right; the tricky part is distinguishing one from the other.

Dealing on the Outside

Dealing is the other side of doing, its external manifestation. Sometimes it is called "doing the deal" or "wheeling and dealing" (although these suggest the too-common disconnection of the dealing from the doing, as when a CEO negotiates an acquisition and then dumps its ill-considered consequences on others). Managers do deals with outsiders, such as suppliers and banks, but also with other managers inside their own organizations.

Doug Ward, who headed up the Canadian Broadcasting Corporation's radio station in Ottawa, noted about the CBC: "This place has become very entrepreneurial, much more deal oriented," with a philosophy of "If you can help me, I'll help you."

There are two main components of the dealing role: *building coalitions* around specific issues (*mobilizing support*)

and using these coalitions with established networks to conduct negotiations. We shall discuss them together.

Much doing requires dealing: to get projects going usually involves considerable negotiating—with suppliers, customers, partners, government officials, and many others.

As head of Hawkshead Films, Carol Haslam had to put together projects across TV networks, sometimes around the world, pitching ideas to her potential clients and convincing them of her firm's ability to execute them. This involved a great deal of connecting and juggling.

Managing partners of consulting firms as well as chief executives of high-technology firms such as a Boeing or an Airbus often act as salespeople to secure contracts with customers. Here they are carrying out what is considered to be operating work in most other industries. But, as noted, sometimes only they have the status and authority to close the deal. **As figureheads, managers add credibility to the negotiations; as nerve centers, they bring comprehensive information to bear on them; in positions of authority, they are able to commit the necessary resources in real time.**

Too Much Micromanaging?

We can conclude this discussion of the action plane by returning to the issue discussed earlier of micromanaging versus macroleading. **Macroleading may well be the bigger problem today. Managers who don't do and deal can become incapable of making sensible decisions and robust strategies.** We no more need managers who never do and deal than we need managers who only do and deal. As we shall now discuss, all around every manager the world of action has to connect to the world of people and both to the world of information.

WELL-ROUNDED MANAGING

I noted at the outset of this chapter that many of the best-known writers in management have emphasized one aspect of managing to the exclusion of the others. Now it can be appreciated why each of them is wrong: heeding the advice of any one of them can (with reference to the diagram of our model) encourage a lopsided practice of managing. Like an unbalanced wheel at resonant frequency, the job risks oscillating out of control.

Accepting Tom Peters's emphasis on doing can cause a centrifugal explosion of the job, as it flies off in all directions, free of the anchoring effect of a strong frame at the center. Opting instead for Michael Porter's view of the manager as analyzer, who focuses on formulating strategy at the center, can encourage centripetal implosion, as the job closes in on itself, far from the tangible actions needed to inform and root strategies. **Thinking is heavy—too much of it can wear a manager down—while acting is light—too much of that and the manager cannot stay put.**

Moreover, **too much leading can result in a job free of content—aimless, frameless, and actionless—while too much linking can produce a job detached from its roots—it becomes public relations. The manager who only communicates never gets anything done, while the manager who only "does" ends up doing it all alone. And the manager who only controls risks controlling an empty shell of "yes" men and**

women. We don't need people-oriented, information-oriented, or action-oriented managers; we need managers who operate on all three planes.

A corny metaphor might make for some good advice here: **The manager has to practice a well-rounded job.** Sure, the roles can sometimes substitute for each other—for example, by pulling employees via leading instead of pushing them through controlling. There are different ways to get this job done. But all the roles must be blended in every managerial job.

We have all experienced lopsided managing, whether due to the detachment of strategizing, the heavy-handedness of controlling, or the self-absorption of narcissistic leading. That is why the model of this chapter has been shown on a single page: as a reminder that this is one job, which has to be *seen* holistically.

Figure 5 lists various competencies associated with the roles discussed in this chapter. Can any manager master all of them? The short answer is no. But as we shall discuss in Chapter 6, the world has been functioning pretty well with managers who, like the rest of humanity, are flawed. We have no other choice.

Achieving Dynamic Balance

When a pill becomes active, its different layers decompose and blend into each other. So, too, for this model: **When managers manage, the distinctions between these roles blur at the margins.** In other words, it may be easy to separate such roles in theory, but that does not mean they can always be distinguished in practice.

Does this negate the model? Not any more than the blending of the layers of a pill during digestion negate the need for its

FIGURE 5   Competencies of Managing

A. Personal Competencies
1. Managing self, internally (reflecting, strategic thinking)
2. Managing self, externally (time, information, stress, career)
3. Scheduling (chunking, prioritizing, agenda setting, juggling, timing)

B. Interpersonal Competencies
1. Leading individuals (selecting, teaching/mentoring/coaching, inspiring, dealing with experts)
2. Leading groups (team building, resolving conflicts/mediating, facilitating processes, running meetings)
3. Leading the organization/unit (building culture)
4. Administering (organizing, resource allocating, delegating, authorizing, systematizing, goal setting, performance appraising)
5. Linking the organization/unit (networking, representing, collaborating, promoting/lobbying, protecting/buffering)

C. Informational Competencies
1. Communicating verbally (listening, interviewing, speaking/presenting/briefing, writing, information gathering, information disseminating)
2. Communicating nonverbally (seeing [visual literacy], sensing [visceral literacy])
3. Analyzing (data processing, modeling, measuring, evaluating)

D. Actional Competencies
1. Designing (planning, crafting, visioning)
2. Mobilizing (firefighting, project managing, negotiating/dealing, politicking, managing change)

Source: Compiled from various sources; adapted from Mintzberg (2004:280).

different ingredients. To understand the practice of managing, we need to understand each of its component parts, even if they cannot always be executed distinctly. For example, Andy Grove, as CEO of Intel, has described "nudging" at the interfaces of leading, controlling, communicating, and doing:

> You often do things at the office designed to influence events slightly, maybe making a phone call to an associate

suggesting that a decision be made in a certain way. . . . In such instances you may be advocating a preferred course of action, but you are not issuing an instruction or a command. Yet you're doing something stronger than merely conveying information. Let's call it "nudging" because through it you nudge an individual or a meeting in the direction you would like. This is an immensely important managerial activity in which we engage all the time, and it should be carefully distinguished from decision-making that results in firm, clear directives. In reality, for every unambiguous decision we make, we probably nudge things a dozen times. (1983:51–52)

Concerning the blending and mixing of the managerial roles, consider Fabienne Lavoie's day on the nursing ward.

The remarkable thing was how everything just flowed in a natural rhythm. I could find clear examples of each of the roles, yet she mixed them in such short snatches that they all just blended together. A short conversation with a nurse seemed to combine subtle controlling with sympathetic leading; then she was on the telephone with a patient's relative (linking); all the while, she was constantly doing, yet that was difficult to distinguish from her leading and her communicating.

Earlier, I described the controlling of insiders and the convincing of outsiders. But insiders who are highly skilled, such as researchers in a laboratory, often need to be convinced more than controlled by their managers. And captive suppliers of a company can sometimes be controlled like insiders. The vertical lines from "superiors" to "subordinates" have been weakening in many organizations, while the horizontal lines to partners and colleagues have been strengthening.

To insist that all managers have to perform all the roles in the model—swallow the whole pill—is not to suggest that managers do not favor some roles over others. Every job has specific needs to which its manager has to respond. Moreover, each manager exhibits his or her own style, as we shall discuss in the next chapter. Accordingly, **effective managers do not exhibit perfect balance among the roles, but rather a dynamic balance across them, as they tilt back and forth between them.**

It is this dynamic balance that renders futile the teaching of management in a classroom, especially one role or one competency at a time. Even mastering all the competencies do not a competent manager make. No simulation I have ever seen in a classroom—case, game, in-basket exercise—comes remotely close to replicating the job itself. Management has to be learned on the job.

Practicing managers can certainly benefit from coming into a classroom that encourages them to reflect, alone and together, on the experience they have acquired on the job (as we shall discuss in Chapter 6). But that experience can be so varied, as we shall discuss next, that the focus of such a classroom has to be more on the managers learning from their own experience than on the professors teaching them about theories.

4 Managing Every Which Way

The untold varieties of managing

No one size fits all in managing; there is no "one best way" to manage. Indeed, to repeat, people who believe themselves prepared to manage everything in general are often able to manage nothing in particular. Managing is very much rooted in context. Spend a few hours with a variety of managers, and you will likely be struck by how varied this job can be: a bank chairman visiting branches; a Red Cross delegate looking for tensions in a refugee camp; an orchestra conductor in rehearsal and then performance; the head of an environmental NGO engaging in formal planning while fighting off a political challenge. **Managing is almost as varied as life itself, because it is about so much that happens in life itself.**

The last two chapters looked at the common characteristics and content of managing. This one considers its sheer variety. How to find order in the variety we see?

The main sources of variety discussed here are the external context (national culture, sector, industry); the form of the organization (entrepreneurial, professional, etc.) as well as its age and size; the job's level in the hierarchy and the work supervised; temporary pressures of the job; and the person in the job (background, tenure, personal style).

MANAGING—ONE PRACTICE AT A TIME

The inclination, in both research and practice, has been to try to understand managing one of these factors at a time. For example, how does managing at the "top" differ from that in the "middle," or doing it in government compared with in business, or in China compared with in India? But when I considered the twenty-nine days of managing that I studied, I was surprised to find how insignificant, and sometimes even ambiguous, many of these common factors were in most of these jobs:

Did it much matter that Bramwell Tovey, as conductor of the Winnipeg Symphony, was British or conducting in Canada? He was a "top" manager, yet also a first-line supervisor, since this was a small organization. And how about his personal style? That was a factor—it's always a factor—but about how Bramwell managed more than what he did as manager. He conducted the orchestra, much like other conductors. The two factors that did seem particularly explanatory were the industry (namely, the fact that this was a symphony orchestra) and the form of organization (one of highly trained professionals).

I concluded that, while we cannot dismiss any of these factors, since each appears to have had a strong influence on *some* of these days of managing, **what we can dismiss is the effort to understand managing one factor at a time. These factors thus have to be considered together, one practice at a time.**

The first section of this chapter looks briefly at evidence about each of these factors, while the second focuses on one factor in particular, personal style. The third considers the factors together, in terms of the postures that managers seem to adopt (e.g., "maintaining the workflow" or "managing out of the middle"). And the final section discusses "managing beyond the manager."

THE EXTERNAL CONTEXT OF MANAGING

Every managerial job is situated in some external context—namely, its cultural milieu, its sector in general, and its industry in particular.

The Outside Culture

Many of us like to think that we live in a place of unique culture, with its own prevalent managerial style. Yet a number of studies have found striking similarities in the practice of management across cultures. Culture certainly matters, but we are inclined to exaggerate our differences. In the twenty-nine days of my study, I found culture to be a compelling factor in only two:

Abbas Gullet and Stephen Omollo were in the Red Cross Camps in Tanzania because of the tragic events that had taken place just across the border, in Rwanda. This had a major effect on their managing, causing them to be supersensitive about security and so emphasizing the role of controlling. Contrast this with the two Australians I observed at the Greenpeace headquarters in Amsterdam, who could have been doing their job anywhere, since Greenpeace's cultural milieu is the whole world. John Cleghorn, as head of the Royal Bank of Canada, and Max Mintzberg, co-founder of a chain of telephone stores in Montreal, had vastly different days despite both being Canadian.

The Sector

The twenty-nine managers came from all the sectors: business, government, health care, and the plural sector (NGOs, etc.). Is this a key to understanding managerial work?

There were certainly competitive (economic) pressures in all the private sector organizations of my study, but these seemed significant in only three of the six days. In the public sector, intensive political pressures were evident in only one of the nine days. In fact, the most intensive politics were encountered in the days with Rony Brauman of Doctors Without Borders and Paul Gilding, executive director of Greenpeace, both in the plural sector. In health care, the professional nature of the work was clearly influential for the managers close to the operations, but less so for those in higher reaches of the hierarchy (as will be discussed later). One message of this seems to be that treating one sector as superior—"business knows best"—hardly makes sense when management practice in business itself varies so widely.

The Industry

Using the term *industry* in a broad sense (e.g., the "orchestra industry"), we see that there is obviously a wide range of industries in which managers work. This factor figured prominently in twelve of the twenty-nine days—for example, filmmaking in Carol Haslam's day and orchestra conducting in Bramwell Tovey's day. But the effect of industry was strongest for the first-line managers, closest to the workers and the users, less so for those at middle and senior levels.

THE NATURE OF THE ORGANIZATION

Here we look at various characteristics related to organizing: the form of the organization, its age and size, the level of the job in the hierarchy, and the work it supervises.

The Form of Organization

It is interesting that the kind of organization proved to be the most prominent factor by far—in twenty of the twenty-nine days—for understanding what the managers of this study did. Yet this factor is commonly ignored. Why?

Imagine biology with no vocabulary to discuss species: how to distinguish, for example, beavers from bears without any word beyond mammal? This is the state we are in when it comes to organizations; we have little vocabulary beyond the word "organization." How is a chief executive to explain to a consultant or a board member that "You are treating us like an X kind of organization, but we are really a Y kind of organization" when there are no commonly understood words for X and Y?

In earlier work,[2] I proposed six basic forms of organization:

Entrepreneurial organization: centralized around a single leader, who engages in considerable doing and dealing

Machine organization: formally structured, with simple repetitive operating tasks, its managers engaging in a considerable amount of controlling

Professional organization: built around professionals who do the operating work, largely on their own, while the managers focus more externally, on linking and dealing to support and protect the professionals

Project organization (adhocracy): built around project teams of experts that innovate, with the project managers concentrating on leading to build the teams, doing to aid the project work, and linking to connect the different teams, while the senior managers engage in linking and dealing to bring in new projects

Missionary organization: dominated by a strong culture, with the managers emphasizing leading to enhance and sustain that culture

Political organization: dominated by conflict, with the managers sometimes having to emphasize doing and dealing in the form of firefighting

These inclinations were evident in filmmaking (project organization) and retailing (entrepreneurial organization), but **the strongest impact of organization on managing showed up in**

---

[2] Introduced in Mintzberg (1979 and 1983) and most accessible in 1989 (Part II; see also Mintzberg 2007: Chapter 12 on how each form tends to create its strategies).

the professional organizations, especially for their managers
close to the operating professionals—for example, managers
of nursing, medicine, and the orchestra.

The Age and Size of the Organization

We might expect managing in small and young organizations to
be more intense and less formalized. Not so fast.

*True, Max Mintzberg was managing intensely in a small,
young retail chain, while John Cleghorn managed in a more
formalized way with a large, mature bank. On the other
hand, an orchestra is a small organization, even if composed
of one large unit, and the newest of them conform to centuries of formalized protocol. The huge size of the National
Health Service of England certainly influenced the work of
its chief executive, but would the work of its medical and
nursing managers have been much different had they been
in independent hospitals, even small ones?*

The Level in the Hierarchy

Level refers to the location of the job in the formal hierarchy of
authority—"top," "middle," and first-line supervision at the base
(never called "bottom"!). All of this, of course, refers to the location
on a chart printed on a piece of paper. **Don't necessarily go
looking for middle management in the middle of anything,
or top management "on top of things."**

We generally believe that the higher a manager's level, the more
unstructured and long-range the job. So, as noted in Chapter 1, why

was Gord Irwin in the Front Country Office of the Banff National Park so concerned with the environmental impact of a parking lot, while Norm Inkster, as head of the RCMP, was watching clips of the previous day's newscasts to avoid embarrassing questions to his minister in Parliament that day? Managers do what they have to do, not what the theory tells them to do. Who else in the RCMP could have done what Norm Inkster did that day?

As for middle management, it has been under attack for some years now, accused of having been bloated and therefore subjected in many corporations to repeated "downsizings"—a contemporary form of bloodletting, the cure for every corporate ill. How come so many companies discovered the problem all at once? Were their senior managers that inattentive before—or after?

Once again, the simple generalities don't work. As Quy Huy of Insead has put it, **middle managers are often "far better than most senior executives . . . at leveraging the informal network . . . that makes substantial, lasting change possible."** They know "where the problems are" yet can also "see the big picture" (2001:73.).

Doug Ward, manager of the CBC radio station in Ottawa, sat between the tangible operations of radio programming and the intricacies of the corporation's formal hierarchy. "It's nice having a job at the interface," he said. Thanks to his earlier experience (he had been head of the entire radio network), Doug could challenge the rest of the organization and act in ways beneficial to it—for example, by helping to create a new radio program later adopted by the network.

The Work Supervised

If chief executives manage whole organizations, then what do other managers manage? Functions, projects, and staff groups, among other things.

The word *function* has mostly been used to describe the classic components of business: production, marketing, sales, and so forth. But function has to be seen in a more generic way, as one component in a chain of operating activities: sales in a manufacturing firm is a function because it cannot stand alone, just as is nursing or medicine in a hospital. Function figured significantly in seven of the twenty-nine days I studied.

THE TEMPORARY PRESSURES OF MANAGING

Next we come to the conditions of the moment, the situation at hand: a strike, a merger, a lawsuit, a sudden competitive attack, and so forth.

We know from long-standing research that crises—imminent bankruptcy, sudden hostilities, collapse of a currency—can cause an organization to centralize power, so that one person is able to act quickly and decisively, especially in the roles of *doing* and *controlling.*

Surprising is that these temporary pressures seemed prominent in only seven of the twenty-nine days. Does this negate the earlier finding that managers are real-time responders to the pressures at hand? I think not. Rather, the pressures of managing are often not temporary at all, but perpetual. In other words, pressure in this job is business as usual. For example, Brian Adams of Bombardier was not in a classical job of "management by exception"; his was a job of the management of exceptions.

Worth a brief mention here is fashion as a temporary factor. Much like political correctness, there is "managerial correctness"—the fashionable way to practice management at some given time. Here we find the flavor of the managerial month, so to speak (the expression itself having been the flavor of a few managerial months)—for example, over the years with regard to managing people: human relations, participative management, Theory Y, quality of work life, total quality management, empowerment.

Such fashion can influence managerial work temporarily, at least for those managers inclined to follow the crowd. There are also fashionable managerial styles—for example, the "heroic leadership" now so prevalent at the CEO level. But fashion was not much in evidence in the twenty-nine days I observed; in contrast, as noted, was Bramwell Tovey conforming to a historical tradition in the field of orchestral music.

THE PERSON IN THE JOB

By far the greatest attention among all the factors has been accorded to managers' "styles"—namely, how they approach their work, beyond the demands of the job and the organization, et cetera. Style, in other words, is about how the incumbent *makes* the job, as opposed to just *doing* the job. Thus, President Truman "loved to make decisions," which he did quickly, while President Eisenhower was "disposed" to keep away from them (Dalton 1959:163).

Is style the result of character or of experience, nature or nurture? The answer, of course, has to be both. We shall first discuss nurture, in the form of the manager's background and tenure. Then we shall consider different personal styles of managing, whether influenced by nature or nurture.

The Manager's Background

A manager's background can pertain to education, earlier positions, successes and failures, and other experiences. While background obviously influenced all twenty-nine managers of this study, it seemed significant in only six cases, all but one due to education: John Tate at the Canadian Justice Department, with his background in law, and Ann Sheen, Fabienne Lavoie, and Drs. Thick and Webb, all with professional backgrounds in nursing or medicine.

The Manager's Tenure

Tenure in the job, the organization, and the industry was found to be a significant factor in nine cases. For example:

Abbas Gullet joined the Red Cross in his youth, attended international conferences in his teens, and later worked in its central headquarters. And so he knew the institution intimately, which was evident especially in how he served as a bridge between the operating site in Tanzania and the headquarters in Geneva. Paul Gilding of Greenpeace and Sandy Davis of the Canadian parks, both not long in their jobs, favored formal planning. Can we conclude that managers rely on such planning to get a sense of a new job? Perhaps only sometimes, because Alan Whelan of BT, also new to his job, did not seem so inclined.

Some Personal Styles of Managing

Think of all the personal styles that are possible in managing—for example, people oriented or task oriented, inclined to change or to maintain continuity, long term or short term. We cannot possibly discuss them all, so I shall focus on three that strike me as especially significant: how proactive is the manager; whether the manager sees him- or herself on top, in the center, or throughout; and whether the manager tilts toward art, craft, or science in practicing management.

Proactiveness. Interestingly, **if one factor stood out in these days of observation, it was proactiveness: the extent to which the managers used whatever degrees of freedom they could seize to drive change or to reinforce stability.** Abbas Gullet, for example, was about as proactive as any manager in this study, but for purposes of stabilizing the refugee camps, while Alan Whelan sought to drive change at BT. What struck me was the propensity of a number of the twenty-nine managers to act in the face of great constraints:

> *Peter Coe, district general manager in the difficult structure of the National Health Service of England, was a prime example. Above him was its vast hierarchy, while below, much of the activity he was supposed to manage was removed from his direct control (independent physicians, hospitals from which his district was supposed to "purchase" services, etc.). The frame of his job was rather vague, and while it seemed to be imposed, in fact, on the day observed, Peter appeared to be profoundly proactive.*

On the Top, in the Center, or Throughout. Another dimension that seems key is where the manager sees him- or herself in relation to others in the unit.

Some managers *see* themselves on top—of the hierarchy of authority—but also metaphorically: above those who report to them, and so likely to give considerable attention to the role of controlling.

Other managers see themselves in the center, of a hub, with activities revolving around them. This seemed true for a number of the women in my study. In *The Female Advantage: Women's Ways of Leadership*, Sally Helgesen wrote that women managers "usually referred to themselves as being in the middle of things. Not on top, but in the center; not reaching down, but reaching out" (1990:45–46). The sharpest gender difference came out in two of the days I spent in Paris, discussed in the accompanying box.

▊ THE YIN AND YANG OF MANAGING

Rony Brauman was head of Doctors Without Borders, and Catherine Joint-Dieterle was in charge of the fashion museum, both in Paris. Both occupied tiny offices and commuted on two wheels, but very different ones—a motorcycle in one case, a scooter in the other, reflecting the pace of their work. Both were deeply involved, but one was far less driven, so to speak.

Doctors Without Borders runs around the world dealing with crises on an intermittent basis. It goes where the world is sick, trying to cure it, or at least palliate it, and then leaves. The fashion museum in Paris stays put and collects heirlooms, which it may hold forever.

Managing followed suit (on these days, at least), in one case, intensive and aggressive, like yang; in the other, nurturing and infusive, like yin.

Doctors Without Borders is not just *about* medicine but *like* medicine. It makes its decisions decisively—to treat a crisis or withdraw
treatment from it—and it prefers the acute to the chronic, tending
to leave when the condition stabilizes. Not coincidentally, it had
a physician as its chief. On the day observed, Rony, too, practiced
management like medicine—as interventionist cure. His work this
day was largely external—racing around Paris for media interviews
to promote a political perspective about the country in which the
organization was working.

The museum conserved both garments and a legacy. Its leader
was tellingly labeled its "Chief Conservator," and her work this day
was more internal, much of it doing, in a detailed way. She operated
with her hands on, literally as well as figuratively. When she talked
about the intimate relationship of clothes to the body, she might
well have used this as a metaphor for the relationship of the organization's mission to its own body—namely, to preserve the heritage
of French clothing within its carefully woven structure.

We are told that yin and yang, these two "great cosmic forces,"
cannot exist without each other. In the duality is found the unity:
there has to be light in the shadows and shadow in the light. If harmony is achieved when yin and yang are balanced, then is there
some rebalancing to be achieved in much of managing?

**Then there are the managers who see themselves, not on
top of a hierarchy or at the center of some kind of hub, so
much as throughout a web of activities.** We talk a lot about
organizations as networks these days—webs of interactive activities. Well, picture that, as in Figure 6, and ask yourself where the
manager belongs in such a structure. On top? A manager on top
of a network is out of it. In the center? A manager in the center
of a network *centralizes* it—that is, draws its communication
patterns toward him- or herself.

FIGURE 6   **Perceptions of the Place of the Manager**

The Manager on Top (of a Hierarchy)

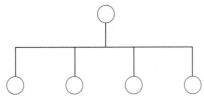

The Manager in the Center (of a Hub)

The Manager Throughout (a Web)

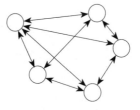

So to manage a network, as in a project organization, the manager has to function throughout—and see him- or herself that way. In other words, the manager has to be everywhere. This suggests favoring linking over leading, dealing over doing, and convincing over controlling.

Styles as Art, Craft, Science. As a framework to identify different styles of managing, I prefer the art-craft-science triangle introduced in Chapter 1. As shown in Figure 7, close to science is what can be called a *cerebral* style—deliberate and analytical. It has long been influential in business, perhaps now more than ever. Close to art is what can be called an *insightful* style—concerned with ideas and visions, intuitive in nature. And close to craft is what can be called an *engaging* style—hands-on and helpful, rooted in experience.

Excessive attention to any one of these styles can lead to imbalanced managing. As also shown in Figure 7, the cerebral style can become *calculating* (too heavy on the science—on analysis), the insightful style *narcissistic* (art for its own sake),

FIGURE 7   **Styles of Managing in Terms of Art, Craft, Science**

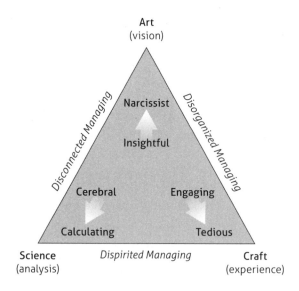

and the engaging style *tedious* (managers hesitating to venture beyond their own experience). Even a combination of two of these styles without the third can be problematic, as shown on the three lines of the triangle: a *disorganized* style (no science), a *disconnected* style (no craft), and a *dispiriting* style (no art).

So the place to be is inside the triangle: **Effective managing requires some blend of art, craft, and science, whether in the person of the manager alone, or else in a management team that works together.** In other words, **management may not be a science, but it does need some of the order of science, while being rooted in the practicality of craft, with some of the zest of art.** An instrument I developed with Beverley Patwell, a consultant in British Columbia, can help to consider your own style, and those of your colleagues (Figure 8).

FIGURE 8 **Assessing Your Personal Style of Managing in Terms of Art, Craft, Science**

Consider how you manage in your job. Circle one of the three words from each row that best describes it. When you are finished, add up how many you have circled in each of the three columns. (Together they should add up to 10.)

The first column represents art, the second craft, the third science.

insightful	engaging	calculating
Ideas	Experiences	Facts
Intuitive	Practical	Analytical
Heart	Hands-on	Head
Strategies	Processes	Outcomes
Inspiring	Engaging	Informing
Passionate	Helpful	Reliable
Novel	Realistic	Determined
Imagining	Learning	Organizing
Seeing it	Doing it	Thinking it
"The possibilities are endless!"	"Consider it done!"	"That's perfect!"

Total Scores

art   craft   science

Source: Developed by © Henry Mintzberg and Beverly Patwell, 2008.

Putting Style in Its Place. I described Carol Haslam's day in the film company as hard dealing and soft leading. The nouns are about *what* she did, the adjectives about *how* she did it. A manager is asked for help from a report. The answer can come as the what, in terms of role: "Why not see Sally on this?" (communicating). Or "Leave it with me" (doing). And within each of these can be the how. For example, concerning the communicating response, "In my experience, Sally will be skittish on this" is quite different from "Tell Sally we miss her—it will help."

So how did personal style affect those twenty-nine days? A lot less than might be expected. While personal style influenced *how* all of these managers did their work, it seemed to have had surprisingly limited effect on *what* that work was. Nursing manager Ann Sheen was quick; GSI president Jacques Benz was reflective; Catherine Joint-Dieterle was yin and Rony Brauman was yang. But when I went back over the twenty-nine days and asked myself if these hows were a major determinant of what the managers did that day, with a few exceptions the answer was no.

Carol Haslam's dealing may have been hard and her leading soft, but would we have expected the head of another similar film company to have concentrated on different roles? And how about Bramwell Tovey: did personal predisposition have much effect on what he did, on or off the podium?

Why should this have been so, given that so much attention has been devoted to managerial styles? Because **what you do as a manager is mostly determined by what you face as a manager, which is not independent of who you are as a person.**

Bramwell Tovey went into music, and from there to a con-
ductor job, because of his natural disposition. Norm Inkster
was no doubt attracted to the RCMP because of its culture
and became head of it in good part because he resonated so
well with that culture.

Of course, who you are helps determine what you get to face. Carol Haslam was not coincidentally in a job that required considerable external dealing, and nursing manager Fabienne Lavoie in a job that required intensive internal leading. (Imagine Carol and Fabienne in each other's jobs.)

Let me reiterate. **Personal style is important, no question. But that seems to be more about *how* managers do things, including the decisions they make and the strategies they shape, than *what* they do as managers.**

Is the Manager a Chameleon? In a *Harvard Business Review* article entitled "Leadership That Gets Results," Daniel Goleman claimed that, much like "the array of clubs in a golf pro's bag," managerial styles can be picked and chosen "based on the demands of the shot. . . . The pro senses the challenge ahead, swiftly pulls out the right tool, and elegantly puts it to work. That's how high impact leaders operate too" (2000:80).

I disagree. The assumption, that we can change our behaviors the way we change our golf clubs—a long-standing one in much of applied psychology and management development—needs to be scrutinized.

Consider Marc, executive director of a hospital. Looking out, he was an advocate for his institution, lobbying for it with apparent effectiveness. But turning around and looking in, Marc himself faced a whole host of advocates, all concerned for their own interests. So the very style that made him effective externally may have caused him problems internally. Unless, of course, he could have pulled out a different club—in the more common metaphor, changed his colors, like a chameleon. The tough, aggressive, advocate—"authoritative," "pacesetting"—merely had to become, say, "affiliative," "democratic" (in terms of the styles Goldman presented). Unfortunately for him, however, this was not a question of putting away a driver in favor of a putter so much as switching from boxing to badminton.

Bear in mind that while chameleons change colors, they do not change habitats. In fact, all they really do is hide. It may work for them in a limited context, but for how long can that work for managers? **The effective manager may be the one whose natural style fits the context more than the one who changes style to fit the context (let alone the so-called professional manager whose style is supposed to fit all contexts).**

No doubt we can all adapt somewhat. But only within limits. Terribly destructive, despite its current popularity, is the belief that the organization has to adapt to the style of its chief executive. This can ride roughshod over important aspects of the organization, such as its culture. **Expecting the incumbent to conform rigidly to the needs of the managerial job may be bureaucratic, but allowing the incumbent carte blanche to *make* the job whatever he or she pleases is no better.** So while every manager has to *make* the job, he or she also has to *do* the job.

A professor of education once asked me what I thought about the current American practice of appointing retired army officers to head up school systems. Good idea, I replied, so long as the country is prepared to have retired school principals run the army.

POSTURES OF MANAGING

As we have seen throughout this chapter, the various contexts of managing are not independent so much as interwoven. In Max Mintzberg's case, for example, a young, small, and competitive business with an entrepreneurial form of organization allowed its chief executive somewhat wide scope to act, but it also generated considerable pressures in the job, leading to a hectic pace with lots of doing and dealing—all of which fitted Max's nature quite well. If we wish to develop a robust understanding of the varieties of managing (for the purposes of selecting, developing, and assessing managers, etc.), we will need a coherent classification of the postures of managing that combine these contexts. Using what I saw in those twenty-nine managerial days, I developed one such classification, comprising twelve postures, as described in the following sections.

Maintaining the Workflow

A number of the managers clearly focused on maintaining the basic workflow to ensure that the operations proceeded smoothly. **Such managers maintain a dynamic balance to keep the**

organization on course, a posture which is more about fine-tuning than major renewing. We might expect this posture of front-line managers in machine organizations (Stephen Omollo in the refugee camps), but I also saw it in professional organizations (Fabienne Lavoie in the hospital), even at the middle management level (Abbas Gullet in the refugee camps), and that of chief executives (Bramwell Tovey maintaining the basic flow of the music).

This is "hands-on" managing, craft in nature, with *doing* the key role, although *communicating* is significant—to catch anything that might go off course.

Connecting Externally

At the other extreme is a posture that connects out more than controls in. In formal terms, **these managers maintain the boundary condition of their organization.** We might expect this especially at senior levels, and saw it with Rony Brauman of Doctors Without Borders, Carole Haslam of Hawkshead Films, and Marc of the hospital—all organizations of knowledge workers. The focus of this posture is obviously on the external roles of *linking* and *dealing*; here we find the negotiators par excellence, also the most enthusiastic networkers. There is a good deal of art in this posture.

Blending All Around

This third posture includes aspects of the first two, and more. These managers were close to the workflow but also connected significantly to the outside world, and most importantly, blended them together.

We might expect this to be a posture of chief executives, but it did not come out that way. **Most were in middle management—perhaps the best place to integrate an organization's activities. All but one were heavily involved in project work,** which can be rather self-contained and requiring rather complete management.

Because of the importance of their lateral relationships, these managers could not afford to see themselves as being on top, or even in the center, so much as throughout: they had to reach out and work through extensive networks. In fact, superiors and subordinates can easily get mixed together with associates and partners in this posture, as was noted in the work of Brian Adams at Bombardier.

This is a posture of connections among the roles, but key ones include *dealing* and *doing* alongside much *communicating.* This posture seems closest to the craft style of managing—more facilitating than directing.

Remote Controlling

The next three postures describe different ways in which especially senior managers of large organizations try to penetrate their hierarchies, to put their stamp on the organization.

Remote controlling **describes a posture of managing that is rather "hands-off," functioning analytically on the information plane.** Managers here see themselves on top, and favor the *controlling* role, whether by making decisions themselves, or by deeming the expected performance of others.

Paul Gilding was new at the helm of Greenpeace, and he seemed to be trying to use formal planning to bring things under control. Ironically while he was encouraging others to engage in more hands-on doing, Paul was consciously avoiding it himself (despite being vigorously urged by one staffer on the day observed to do it).

We might expect remote controlling at the top of large, machine-like organizations, but I saw it in the work of Drs. Webb and Thick at the base of their hospitals, too. Both were part-time managers, more involved with their clinical and/or research activities (where they exhibited more of a craft orientation). So on the days observed, they did their managing rather briefly, in good part by authorizing the decisions of others in the *controlling* role.

Fortifying the Culture

Also especially for senior managers, but very different, comes this posture of art and craft, through personal engagement rather than impersonal control. **The object of this posture is to fortify the culture of the organization—its sense of community—so that people can be trusted to function appropriately.**

Leading is the key role here, reinforced by a good deal of *communicating,* combined with *linking* to protect the organization from external disturbances. These managers likely see themselves at the center of things rather than on top, with the culture swirling all around.

This posture came out most distinctly in the day I spent with Norm Inkster as commissioner of the RCMP—and its consequences were evident in the days I spent with two other officers of the force at middle and operating levels. This was thanks to a combination of factors: a noble mission, a distinguished history, and a chief executive with long tenure and devotion to its culture.

Intervening Strategically

Another senior management posture for penetrating the hierarchy is **personal intervention to drive specific changes.** Jacques Benz exhibited this at GSI by getting involved in projects he believed would have strategic impact, while John Cleghorn at the Royal Bank immersed himself in operating issues about which he was knowledgeable.

The favored role here is obviously *doing*, reinforced by *controlling* and *communicating.* The manager's style is oriented to craft, based on tangible experience. Strategies are thus inclined to emerge more from informal learning than formal planning. And while the manager may be seen as "on top," driving change from "above," he or she tends to be acting throughout, by intervening in many places.

Managing in the Middle

Next we consider managers who sit squarely in the middle of the hierarchy, but adopting two very different postures. Either they go with the flow and manage in the middle, or else they resist it and manage out of the middle.

The classic view sees the middle manager between senior managers in the hierarchy above who formulate strategy and more junior managers below who implement it. **By communicating and controlling on the information plane, the middle manager facilitates the downward flow of strategies and transmits performance information back up the hierarchy.** So there is relatively less doing and dealing, also perhaps less leading. This is a posture of analysis, dependent on planning, budgeting, and other formal systems. It is thus more about maintaining stability than promoting change, with a pace of work that is perhaps less hectic than some other postures, and more formalized.

Managing Out of the Middle

As discussed earlier, there is more to middle management than managing in the middle of a hierarchy. In this posture, I found proactive people managing their way out of the middle.

> *Alan Whelan of BT was certainly in the middle of an extensive hierarchy, a culture in transition, as well as a complicated managerial issue and the ethical dilemma it raised—having to tell a key client that Alan could not get senior management sign-off on their contract while he continued to persuade that management to do so. The latter involved spearheading change in his company by encouraging the senior management to recognize a new world of telecommunications. It is interesting that of all twenty-nine days of observation, twelve of them with chief executives, it was on this day that I heard the most articulate expression of strategy.*[3]

---

[3] To quote Alan's comments to me during the day of observation: "The days of the supplier push of services, to which clients simply subscribed, were long gone. Now business clients wanted services that met their own specific

Managing out of the middle focuses on the external roles of *linking* and *dealing*, making special use of the negotiating skills of the manager. Here were managers who built coalitions to influence people over whom they had no formal authority. I did not see much controlling here or leading—at least not as central preoccupations. This posture, perhaps more than any of the others, exhibited managing closest to art.

Advising from the Side

This is the manager as adviser, specialist, intervener, based on expertise more than authority. **If the *conventional* middle manager sits in midair, then these advising managers sit off to one side, seeking to influence others.** Hence, they are not on top, or even at any center, but can only hope to involve themselves in influential networks.

This may sound like a posture of experts, not managers, but staff units of experts do require managers, who sometimes have to act as experts. Moreover, line managers are sometimes drawn into this advisory role, too. Aside from managing the Canadian Department of Justice, John Tate had to serve as adviser to the minister on issues of policy and legislation.

In this posture, personal style seems to be closer to analysis than art or craft. The roles of *linking* and *communicating* appear

---

needs. Power had moved to the consumer. Network services like those of BT were partial, while the client sought 'end-to-end' services through a single agreement. There was thus a need for integrators to bring together data center, desktop, network, and other services, which required that different suppliers collaborate."

prominent in organizations that tend to be large, stable, and rather formalized—where expert advice is provided internally.

The New Manager

To complete this discussion, two other postures deserve mention, one that is temporary and the other that should be: the new manager and the reluctant manager.

I noted earlier that **the day someone becomes a manager for the first time, everything changes. Yesterday you were doing it; today you are managing it. That can be quite a shock.** Even for an experienced manager in a new job, there is a required time of adjustment. He or she has to develop a network of contacts (*linking*), in order to gain the necessary base of information (*communicating*), which can enable him or her to take action (*doing* and *dealing*).

A thorough discussion of this posture can be found in Linda Hill's book *Becoming a Manager* (2003), whose ideas have been quoted several times in our discussion. Hill pointed out that entering the world of management means maneuvering the abrupt transition from being a specialist and a doer to becoming a generalist and an agenda settler, plus having to shift from acting individually to becoming a network builder who gets things done through others (p. 6).

Hill described how many of the new managers she studied "adopted a hands-on autocratic approach to management" (p. 99), only to discover the limits of their formal authority: "very few people seemed to be following their orders" (p. 100). Thus, these managers "had to learn to lead by persuasion and not by directive" (p. 100) and to discover "new ways to measure success and derive satisfaction from work. It meant evolving an entirely new professional identity" (p. x).

The Reluctant Manager

Two people were, to my mind, reluctant managers—both, in fact, part-time managers in one way or another. Most evident was Dr. Webb, hospital chief of geriatrics, who dispensed with his managerial duties quickly so that he could get on with his clinical work, which he relished:

> *After an intense hour with his "business manager," during which she asked the questions and Dr. Webb gave quick answers, while drinking one cup of coffee after another and smoking a steady chain of cigarettes, he left for his clinical rounds. There he settled down as a calm clinician, responsive to his patients, with time for all their needs, and relaxed with the accompanying staff as well. Coffee and cigarettes were neither consumed nor mentioned during his two hours on the ward.*

> *John Tate at Justice clearly was a manager, although more than that; as noted earlier, he was also an adviser to the minister. But he was also reluctant about his management, and he articulated that clearly.*

Far more numerous were others I studied who relished the job of managing—loved the action, the influence, the pace, all of it. None expressed any real concerns about being a manager, although everyone in this job must complain about it sometimes, even if only to a spouse. This sounds healthy to me. **Managing** is no job to approach with hesitation; it simply requires too much of the total person.

Postures and Purposes for All

While I could associate most of the twenty-nine days of managing with a single posture, it has to be appreciated that all managers adopt most of these postures at some time or other. That is because all these postures reflect basic purposes of managing. **All managers have to connect externally (with all kinds of stakeholders), to maintain the workflow (to keep things on course, even if only in their own offices), and even to control remotely (Who can manage without a budget?). Most have to give attention to fortifying their cultures, promoting strategic initiatives, and acting as experts in their own domain from time to time. And every single manager, no matter where in the hierarchy, has to manage in the middle—of a complex web of influencing forces—which also means that sometimes he or she has to manage out of that middle, too. So to function effectively, every manager not only has to combine all of these postures but also has to blend them all around, even if he or she tends to favor one of the postures, most likely because of the needs of the particular job.**

MANAGING BEYOND THE MANAGER

So far we have taken managing to be rather strictly what managers do. But **always of some importance, and now increasingly** so, is the managing that happens beyond what is done by the people designated as managers.

There are perhaps two reasons for the increased attention to this. One is that, as knowledge work and networks become more prevalent, power over certain kinds of decision making passes naturally to nonmanagers. In the professional organization, for example, most strategies seem to emerge from the venturing efforts of the professionals themselves (see Mintzberg 2007: Chapter 10).

The second reason is that many of us have a love-hate relationship with our managers. Sometimes we see them as the answer to all our problems, and other times we believe they are the cause of all those problems. Most of us, I suspect, adhere to both positions, depending on our latest encounter with a manager.

Beware of both. **We can neither do without managers nor afford to idolize them.** As I hope our discussion to this point has made clear, managers have basic duties to perform in organizations: they provide a sense of unity, consolidate information for action, represent their unit to the outside world, and so on. But **there is much more to organizational purpose, accomplishment, and responsibility than what managers do.**

So on the continuum shown in Figure 9 we should ignore the two extremes—of managers totally in charge at one end and organizations entirely without managers at the other—and consider instead what are labeled in-between maximal managing, participative managing, shared managing, distributed managing, supportive managing, and minimal managing.

FIGURE 9   Managing By and Beyond the Manager

Maximal Managing

In some respects, Henri Fayol (1916, 1949) was right, roughly speaking: there are managers who plan, organize, coordinate, command, and control. Let's call theirs maximal managing, to contrast it with minimal managing.

Is such maximal managing disappearing, as claimed by so many of the gurus of management? Well, look around—at the auto assembly lines, textile factories, supermarkets, call centers, and the abundant clerks in government offices. And don't forget those organizational charts, with that chief on "top." To borrow from Mark Twain, the rumors of the death of maximal managing have been greatly exaggerated. Yet how much managing is really so maximal? Not much.

Participative Managing

An apparent but in fact small step away from maximal managing goes by the label of "participative management," or "empowerment," or "decentralization." Small for the following below:

The problem with participation is that the senior managers who give such power away can easily take it back. As for empowerment, now a fashionable word, **people who have jobs to do shouldn't have to be "empowered" by their managers**—as noted earlier, for example, doctors in hospitals, not to mention bees in hives. And decentralization usually means passing power down a hierarchy from a few senior managers to a few more managers at the next level. That hardly constitutes a serious diffusion of power.[4]

Shared Managing

Here one managerial job is shared among several people. Sometimes it is just two—for example, when a CEO focuses on the external aspects of the job (*linking, dealing*) while a COO (chief operating officer) looks after the internal aspects (*controlling, leading, doing*).

Key to this is the sharing of information. As noted, information is the glue that holds the different managerial roles together. If two people sharing the same job do not fully share their information, problems inevitably ensue.

Team management extends shared management to several people. In one psychiatric hospital (Hodgson, Levinson, and Zaleznik 1965), the chief executive related the organization to its environment (*linking, dealing*) and was assertive; the clinical director managed internal clinical services (*doing, controlling,*

---

[4] In fact, the most famous story of "decentralization" was actually one of centralization, relatively speaking. In the 1920s, Alfred Sloan of General Motors reined in the power of the people running its separate businesses (Chevrolet, Buick, etc.) by creating a divisional structure that subjected them to the performance controls imposed by the headquarters (see Mintzberg 1979:405–406).

leading), and was the supportive one; and a third person dealt with nonroutine innovation (*doing*) and expressed friendship and egalitarian norms (another approach to leading).

One study of a financial institution (Pitcher 1995, 1997) found that its management was balanced among what the author called artists, craftsmen, and technocrats. So long as they worked together, complementing each other's strengths and correcting for each other's weaknesses, the company thrived. But when a technocrat took over and drove out the artists and many of the craftsmen, the company faltered.

Distributed Managing

Distributed managing diffuses responsibility for managing more widely. When geese fly, the leadership changes periodically, as the goose in the front gets tired and falls back. No doubt all the other geese find the one in the lead greatly empowering, perhaps even terribly charismatic—for a while. But if geese can rotate their leadership, and if bees can work vigorously without having to be empowered by the queen (which is our label, not theirs), surely we human beings can achieve such levels of sophistication. In other words, we can treat leadership as something quite natural.

Managerial duties can also be distributed beyond individuals. For example, certain decisions can be made collectively, as in the old New England towns where the members met and voted together. Here, too, the bees do better than most of us today: a key decision, to move the hive from one place to another, is taken collectively. The scout bees survey various sites and return to convey the characteristics of each through their dances. "A contest ensues. Finally the site being advertised most vigorously by the largest number of workers wins, and the entire swarm flies off to it," with the queen joining in (Wilson 1971:548).

Professionals and others in organizations sometimes initiate projects from which major strategies emerge. In an article entitled "Waking Up IBM: How a Gang of Unlikely Rebels Transformed Big Blue," Gary Hamel (2000) recounted the company's entry to e-business. A "self-absorbed programmer" had the initial idea, and finally convinced a staff manager with hardly any resources. The latter stitched together a loose team of people that made it happen. When asked "to whom he reported," that manager replied: 'The Internet.'"

Supportive Managing

If nonmanagers can do more of the managerial roles, then managers themselves can do less. **Consider carefully this form called supportive managing because we are going to be seeing a lot more of it.**

If the queen bee plays no role in that key strategic decision of the hive, then what does she do? Besides a great deal of manufacturing—she produces hordes of baby bees—she does something else that is fundamentally managerial: she emits a chemical substance that holds the hive together. In human organizations, we call this culture, and we have described it under the role of *leading*, as in the case of Norm Inkster of the RCMP.

Bees work largely on their own, without much supervision, as do professors in universities and physicians in hospitals (who often do not even report up the hospital hierarchy). We call such human work "professional," and it requires a different form of managing. "I just didn't get in their way," claimed an ex–business school dean with respect to the professors.

Of course, there is always some need to get in their way—for example, to ensure that budgets get set and met. Moreover, the professionals need support and protection, so that they can accomplish their work with a minimum of disturbance. Hence their managers *link* and *deal* with outside stakeholders to ensure a steady flow of resources, while buffering many of the outside pressures coming in. Robert Greenleaf has called this servant leadership: "individuals . . . are chosen as leaders because" they have a "natural feeling" of wanting "to serve . . . first," compared with the person "who is leader first" (2002:24, 27).

Minimal Managing

The last feasible point on our scale is labeled minimal managing. Here there is hardly anything left to manage, sometimes hardly even an organization as such. But there does remain some coherent activity in need of coordination, from managers.

This may sound curious, until we realize that most of us live with it every day. Think of open source systems such as Wikipedia and the Linux Operating System. These are the ultimate adhocracies, which engage the full creative potential of broad communities. People come and go—they enter, make changes, and exit—but the system carries on—in fact, with remarkable coherence. These are self-managed organizations, almost. Someone had to get them started; someone has to set and enforce the rules of entry, change, and exit; and there is the need to keep the whole thing coherent. That can be done from the background too. On a poster with one duck following a bunch of others is the inscription "There they go. I have to follow them because I am their leader."

This completes our discussion of managing every which way. We have seen immense variation in the practice. The next two chapters build on the first four, considering the inescapable conundrums faced by anyone who takes on the job of managing, and then what it might mean to manage effectively.

5 Managing on Tightropes

The inescapable conundrums of managing

Managing is rife with conundrums. Every way a manager turns, there seems to be some paradox or enigma lurking. Think of these as tightropes on which every manager must walk. "It is precisely the function of the executive . . . to reconcile conflicting forces, instincts, interests, conditions, positions and ideals" (Barnard 1938:21). Notice the use of the word *reconcile*, not *resolve.* This chapter discusses various conundrums at the heart of managing, with some suggestions for reconciliation.

THE SYNDROME OF SUPERFICIALITY

This is perhaps the most basic of all the conundrums of managing, the plague of every manager. **How to get in deep when there is so much pressure to get it done?** As I wrote in my earlier study and noted in Chapter 2, the prime occupational hazard of the manager is superficiality. Because the job is open-ended, the manager is inclined to take on a heavy load of work. As a consequence, as noted, this job does not develop reflective planners so much as it breeds adaptive information manipulators.

"I don't want it good—I want it Tuesday," says a manager. Organizations certainly need to get things done, but must it always be Tuesday? Or right now on e-mail? For example, "speed to market" has become fashionable: get the product out, be first. Why? To recall it?

Managers cannot get rid of superficiality; instead, they have to become proficient at dealing with it—for example, handling complex issues by breaking them into small steps that can be taken one at a time. They also have to hone their capacity to reflect on their work—to find time to step back , and out.

Reflection without action may be passive, but action without reflection is thoughtless. As Saul Alinsky pointed out in his book *Rules for Radicals*, "most people go through life undergoing a series of happenings." These "become experiences when they are digested, when they are reflected on, related to general patterns, and synthesized" (1971:68–69). In our International Masters in Practicing Management (www.impm.org), where the managers spend a good deal of time reflecting on their own and each other's experience, one coined the term "refl'action" to describe this conundrum.

It has been said of great athletes that they see the game just a little bit slower than the other players, and so they can make that last-second maneuver. Perhaps this is also a characteristic of effective managers: faced with great pressure, they can cool it, sometimes just for a moment, to make that thoughtful maneuver.

THE PREDICAMENT OF PLANNING

A variant of the Syndrome of Superficiality is the Predicament of Planning. If the former looks in from the outside, about the pressures to be superficial, then this conundrum looks out from the inside, about **how to plan, strategize, just plain think, let alone think ahead, in such a hectic job.**

This conundrum pits the dynamic characteristics of managing discussed in Chapter 2 (the hectic pace, the interruptions, etc.) against the manager's responsibilities for articulating direction and overseeing decisions made in the unit. This is a conundrum because managers can neither avoid these pressures nor fail to get beyond them.

Does Strategic Planning Resolve This Conundrum?

So what is the harried manager to do? Shut the door? Go off to a retreat? Call a consultant? Sure—sometimes. Just so long as these are recognized as temporary alleviations more than fundamental solutions.

And then there is the most popular prescription of all: strategic planning—the ideal solution for the harassed manager. If you are unable to think ahead and so cannot come up with that strategic vision, let the technique do the visioning for you. (A technique is something you can use in place of a brain.)

Unfortunately, strategic planning never worked as planned—it has never been conducive to developing strategy. Planning offers analysis; strategy requires synthesis. Analysis can certainly feed into synthesis, but it can never substitute for it. When Michael

Porter wrote in *The Economist* that "I favor a set of analytic techniques to develop strategy" (1987), he was dead wrong: nobody ever developed a strategy through a technique. The world of analysis is categorical; the world of strategy is confusing. Sure, analytic techniques can feed into the strategy process. But they cannot be it.

Planning unfolds on schedule while managing has to deal with problems and opportunities as they arise.[5] For example, how was anyone in the Canadian Parks to reconcile "Our mission is to sustain the integrity, health, diversity, majesty and beauty of Western Canada's Cultural and National Heritages" with a knock-down, drag-out battle over the expansion of a parking lot?

Crafting Strategy Instead[6]

In strategic planning, managers are supposed to think in their heads—formulate strategies—so that others can act—implement them. The process is deductive and deliberate—in effect, more science than art or craft.

In our research that tracked the comings and goings of strategies in ten organizations across decades (Mintzberg 2007), we found something else. **Strategies can form without being formulated: they can *emerge* through informal learning, as people discover ideas and establish initiatives that can grow into major strategies.** In other words, the process is

---

[5] All of this has been discussed in my book *The Rise and Fall of Strategic Planning* (1994c; see also 1994a).

[6] The following is drawn from Mintzberg (1987, 2007: Chapter 12) and Mintzberg, Ahlstrand, and Lampel (2009).

inductive—acting drives thinking—just as much as thinking drives acting.

Strategies are not tablets carved on top of mountains, to be carried down for execution. They can be developed on the ground by anyone who has the experience and capacity to see the general beyond the specifics. **Remaining in the stratosphere of concepts is no better for a strategist than having his or her feet firmly planted in concrete.**

This means that managers can alleviate the Predicament of Planning by letting a thousand strategic flowers bloom in their organizations and then selecting those that can best serve it. Such managers eschew a cerebral style of managing, which assumes that strategies are grown in a hothouse, in favor of an engaging style that opens up fields of potential growth.

THE LABYRINTH OF DECOMPOSITION

The world of organizations is chopped into little pieces, some natural, some not: divisions, departments, products, and services, as well as missions, objectives, programs, and budgets. Likewise, agendas are decomposed into issues, and strategic issues are decomposed into strengths, weaknesses, threats, and opportunities.

Overseeing all of this are managers, who are supposed to integrate the whole confusing mess (albeit often of their own making). Hence, we get the Labyrinth of Decomposition: **Where to find synthesis in a world so decomposed by analysis?**

Synthesis is the very essence of managing: putting things together, in the form of coherent visions, unified organizations, and integrated systems. This is what makes managing so difficult—and so interesting. How, then, can a manager see the big picture amid so many little details? It's not as if the organization is a museum with that big picture on some wall. It has to be constructed, in the minds of its people.

Consider that ubiquitous organizational chart, which is supposed to be an orderly portrayal of the components of the organization. It might instead be seen as a labyrinth through which its people have to maneuver. The assumption behind the chart is that if each unit does its job correctly, the whole organization will function smoothly. In other words, structure is supposed to take care of organization, just as planning is supposed to take care of strategy. Anyone who believes this should find a job as a hermit.

Chunking

As noted earlier, Peters and Waterman (1982) have written enthusiastically about "chunking": the manager grabs hold of big problems by breaking them into little chunks that can be dealt with one at a time. That's fine until the manager has to put these chunks back together. It's not as if they fit together in some sort of jigsaw puzzle. This is more like playing with Lego blocks, except that the pieces don't attach very well, and the manager may not be clear about what has to be built.

In a colorful article entitled "The Magic Number Seven, Plus or Minus Two: Some Limits on Our Capacity for Processing Information," George Miller (1956) pointed out that we humans can handle only about seven chunks of information in our short- and intermediate-term memories. So how are we supposed to squeeze that big picture into our little brains?

Painting the Big Picture

Let's look at this metaphor literally. How does a painter see the big picture? Like the manager, there is no place to go to see it—short of copying the big picture of someone else, in which case this person will not be a great painter (any more than a manager who copies other strategies will be a great strategist). **That big picture has to be painted stroke by stroke, experience by experience.** The painter may start with an overall image, but from there the picture has to emerge from a host of little actions. And so, too, do many strategies. Few companies these days have a bigger or better strategy than IKEA, the furniture chain. That is one big corporate picture. It reportedly took fifteen years to paint it.

Natural and Unnatural Managerial Jobs

I began discussion of this conundrum by noting that some of the decomposed chunks of organizations are natural while others are not. **When a manager is put in charge of a chunk that is not natural, the job can become impossible.**

Some units seem rather natural to manage—for example, the IKEA chain, or one store in that chain. Others do not—for example, two stores in the IKEA chain, or a chain of furniture stores combined with a chain of hardware stores. Ann Sheen faced just that: she was in charge of nursing for two hospitals in England, several miles apart. They had been magically merged on a sheet of paper somewhere. What made them one managerial unit? What was natural about managing that?

Arbitrarily designated managerial jobs are all too common. Another of the managers I studied, Sandy Davis, was in charge of the national parks of western Canada. Each park had its own manager. What was her role? In other words, what did a bunch of parks that happened to be in western Canada have in common?

One danger is that the managers of such combinations will feel compelled to find things in common—for example, by calling meetings of the park managers to search for synergies among them. Another is that the managers will micromanage. **Nothing is more dangerous in an organization than a manager with little to do.** Managers are usually energetic people—that is how they got to be managers in the first place, and the more senior they are, the more energetic they tend to be. Put them in jobs where they have little to do, and they will find things to do. Then the trouble starts.

THE QUANDARY OF CONNECTING

The first three conundrums were mostly about thinking, in the managers' heads. The next three are about managing on the information plane.

As noted earlier, a major occupational hazard of managing is to know more and more about less and less until finally the manager knows nothing about everything. The Quandary of Connecting addresses what lies behind this: **How to keep informed—"in touch"—when managing by its own nature removes the manager from the very things he or she is managing?** In other words, how to connect when the job is intrinsically disconnected?

J. Sterling Livingston (1971) of the Harvard Business School wrote about the "second-handedness" of conventional management education—specifically MBA cases. He should have made that third-handedness, because managing itself is second-handed. Organizations are designed so that some people do the basic operating work (designing, producing, selling, etc.), while other people, called managers, oversee it. Management, to repeat, means getting things done through other people, whether that be on the people plane (leading and linking) or the information plane (controlling and communicating). Even on the action plane, managers do and deal largely to enable others to get things done.

Some people claim that detachment can make a manager more objective. True enough. But someone else once remarked that to be objective is to treat people like objects. Is that what we want of our managers? And then there are those who believe that the Internet puts everyone in touch, no matter where they may be. In touch with a keyboard (as noted in Chapter 2), but in touch with the nuances of the organization?

This conundrum is probably least worrisome for the first-line manager, who has natural access to the operations. This struck me especially in the time I spent with Stephen Omollo in the refugee camps, watching him roaming about, picking up information so enthusiastically. At one point, after stopping at the food distribution area, he announced to me that there were no problems this day because no one had come to him to complain. Peters and Waterman (1982) described "management by walking around"; here we had management by just "being there."

Yet ironically, the Quandary of Connecting came out most clearly in the frustration expressed by Gord Irwin, front country manager in the Banff National Park. He found himself squeezed between the tangible realities of the park he knew so well and his new responsibilities embedded in the abstractions of administration. But that frustration was hardly restricted to new managers. Bramwell Tovey was likewise nostalgic about the musical work he left behind.

Slabs Across Silos

Even so, Bramwell, like Steve and Gord, was still close enough to the operation to be able to connect to them naturally. This was a small organization, and, as noted, Bramwell was a "top" as well as a bottom manager.

But the organizations of Steve and Gord were large. In fact, that was the part of Gord's frustration: managers piled atop him and atop each other in the hierarchy of authority. And the higher "up" such managers are, the more detached they are from the operations, to the point where, in the words of Paul Hirsch, the CEO becomes "the lightening rod [sic] for not knowing what's going on."

We all know about the *silos* in organizations—those vertical separations between the functions. As shown in Figure 10, for example, they keep marketing apart from sales and sales apart from production. This conundrum suggests that *slabs* may be a more serious problem. As also shown in Figure 10, the slabs cut across the silos in horizontal layers that isolate managers from each other at different levels in the hierarchy. **When the slabs are especially thick, the Quandary of Connecting can carry the organization into strategic gridlock: the senior managers lack the detailed knowledge, not only to create robust strategies themselves but even to recognize the compelling strategic initiatives that are being created by people at other levels in the organization.** We can say that an *administrative gap* opens

FIGURE 10 **Silos and Slabs in Organizations**

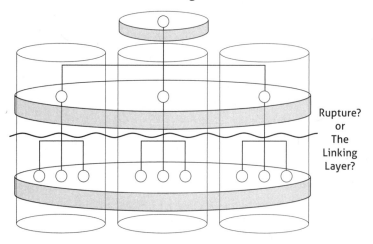

Rupture?
or
The
Linking
Layer?

up, between what happens on the ground, where products and services meet customers, and what gets discussed in the offices of administration.

Getting "In Touch"

How to close this gap? That's easy—in principle. (1) Bring the operating people "up," to connect with the management; (2) take the management people "down," to get in touch with the operations; (3) shrink the gap ("delayer"); or (4) make better use of middle managers to connect up and down.

We discussed the first of these in the last chapter: how non-managers can share the job of managing. As for bringing the managers down, Steve Omollo's "being there" in the camps is illustrative: get the managers out of their offices and into the places where their organization serves its basic purpose—not just to "drop in" but to have personal presence, in body and spirit.

I took my car in for service one day and was chatting with the owner of the dealership when he said something that surprised me: "I don't have an office here." No wonder he was always around, on his feet, much like Fabienne Lavoie in the nursing ward.

The potency of managers being there, in speaking range of others, is not to be underestimated. Of course, not all managers are as lucky as he was, to have most of his organization and customers so close at hand. Even so, why does so much managing have to take place in isolated offices and closed meeting rooms? One Japanese company, Kao, became famous for holding its management meetings in open areas; any employee who went by was welcome to join. Such companies, like that car dealership, do not need an open-door policy!

In our Practicing Management program, a manager from Fujitsu took his class to see the open area where he and his managerial colleagues worked—with no partitions, just desks. "Who's that?" asked a manager from a Canadian bank about someone she saw on his feet, talking to a manager at a desk. "That's our manager," answered our host, pointing out the manager's empty desk, much like the others. "How can you work with your boss looking over your shoulder like that?" she replied in horror. "What's the problem?" he asked. What looked like controlling to her was facilitating to him. This wasn't a manager micromanaging; he was keeping in touch.

Shrinking the gap by reducing the number of slabs, via so-called downsizing, has become popular—too popular and too easy, as noted earlier like bloodletting was in medicine centuries ago. Sure, it can relieve organizations that are bloated with too much middle management. But how often have necessary middle managers been casually dismissed alongside redundant ones?

There can be a better way to close the administrative gap: by making more effective use of middle managers who can connect naturally both ways—to the operations and the abstractions. We can call this the *linking level*, shown in Figure 10.

Many of us believe that "top management" has the capacity to oversee everything. Yet we all know examples of myopia instead, when nothing looks very clear from such a distant vantage point. **Often the linking level of middle managers can be a better place to connect the operating realities with the big strategic picture,** and in the process see management more in the center than on top (see Figure 11).

FIGURE 11   **Managing All Around**

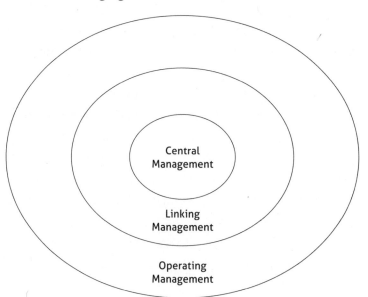

THE DILEMMA OF DELEGATING

Here we reverse the previous conundrum. In that one, managers have trouble connecting because their job takes them out of touch; in this one, managers have difficulty delegating because they are better informed than the people to whom they have to delegate.

Is this a contradiction? Not when we appreciate the nature of the information in question. The manager, as nerve center of the unit, is its most broadly informed member even if not the most specifically informed about any of its specialties. So the manager who is a generalist has to delegate to someone who is a specialist.

There would be no problem if the manager could easily share his or her nerve center information relevant to the delegated task. But often, as noted in Chapter 2, much of this information arrives orally and is therefore stored only in the manager's brain. Even when some can be accessed, transmission can be a time-consuming process. The manager has to "brief" the person orally. So **how is the manager to delegate when so much of his or her information is personal, oral, and often privileged as well?**

Hence, managers seem damned by the nature of their information to a life of either overwork or frustration. In the first case, they do too many tasks themselves or else have to spend too much time sharing their oral information. In the second case, they have to look on as delegated tasks are performed inadequately, by the uninformed (relative to them). It is too common to witness people being blamed for failures because they lacked the information necessary to perform their delegated tasks. Delegating by dumping is not responsible managing.

Managers can relieve this conundrum by sharing their information with people in their unit, especially a second-in-command, as regularly and comprehensively as possible. That way, when it comes time to delegate, at least half the problem is solved.

Does this sharing raise the risk that confidential information will fall into the wrong hands? Sure, sometimes (although refusing to share information is often a smokescreen for hoarding power). But contrast this with the benefits of having well-informed colleagues.

THE MYSTERIES OF MEASURING

It has become a popular adage in some quarters that if you can't measure it, you can't manage it. That's strange, because who has ever reliably measured the performance of management itself? I guess this means that management cannot be managed. Indeed, who has ever even tried to measure the performance of measurement? So we'll have to get rid of measurement, too. Or should we instead face the fact that measurement is loaded with its own conundrums, not the least of which is **how to manage it when you can't rely on measuring it?**

Of course, if measurement were comprehensive and reliable, we wouldn't have to worry about the last two conundrums. Managers could sit in their offices and get fully informed. No need to spend all that time walking around, being there, communicating. And they could also delegate to their heart's content: hit the send button and off goes the information alongside the delegated task. Presumably that is what has made measurement so appealing, especially for managers removed from the tangible activities of their organizations. After all, numbers don't lie, right? The data are reliable, objective, "hard."

The Soft Underbelly of "Hard Data"

What exactly is "hard data"? Rocks are hard, but data? Ink on paper and electrons in a computer are hardly hard. (Indeed, the latter are described as "soft copy"!)

If you must have a metaphor, try instead clouds in the sky. You can see them clearly from a distance, but up close they are more obscure. Once upon them, you can poke your hand through them and feel nothing. "Hard" is the illusion of having turned events and their results into statistics. And these are as clear and unambiguous as clouds. Objective, too. That employee over there is not a cold-hearted egocentric, but a 4.7 on some psychologist's scale. The company didn't just do well; it earned a 16.7 percent return on investment last year. Isn't that clear enough?

Soft data, in contrast, can be fuzzy, ambiguous, subjective. Such data usually require interpretation; most of them can't even be transmitted electronically. In fact, as noted, they may be no more than gossip, hearsay, and impression. How objective is that?

Hence, the dice are loaded. Hard data win every time, at least until they hit the soft material of the human brain. So let's consider the soft underbelly of hard data.

■ *Hard data are limited in scope.* They may provide the basis for description, but often not for explanation. So the profits went up. Why? Because the market was expanding? You can probably get a number on that. Because a key competitor has been doing dumb things? No numbers on that. Because your own management was brilliant? No numbers on that either (so let's assume it's correct). The fact is that we usually require soft data to explain what's behind the hard numbers: politics in the competitor's company, the expression on a customer's face, and so on. In comparison, hard data alone can be sterile, if not impotent. "No matter what I told him," complained one of the subjects of Kinsey's study of sexual behavior in the human male, "he just looked at me straight in the eye and asked 'How many times?'" (in Kaplan 1964).

■ *Hard data are often excessively aggregated.* These data usually comprise lots of facts combined together and then reduced to some aggregate number, such as that quintessential bottom line. Think of all of life that is lost in producing that number. It is fine to see the forest from the trees . . . unless you are in the lumber business. Then you need to know about the trees, too. Too much managing takes place as if from a helicopter, where the trees look like a green carpet.

■ *Much hard information arrives too late.* Information takes time to "harden." Don't be fooled by the speed with which those electrons race around the Internet. Events first have to be documented as "facts" and then aggregated into results and then reports, which may have to await some predetermined schedule (such as the end of a quarter). By that time, competitors may have run off with your customers.

■ *Finally, a surprising amount of hard data is just plain unreliable.* They look good, all those definitive numbers. But where did they come from? Lift up the rock of hard data and see what you find crawling underneath:

> Public agencies are very keen on amassing statistics—they collect them, add them, raise them to the nth power, take the cube root and prepare wonderful diagrams. But what you just never forget is that every one of those figures comes in the first instance from the village watchman,

who just puts down what he damn pleases (attributed to Sir Josiah Stamp 1928, cited in Maltz 1997).

And not just public agencies. Business today is obsessed with numbers. Yet who goes back to find out what the watchmen put down? Moreover, even if the recorded facts were reliable, what is lost in the process of quantification and aggregation? Numbers get rounded up; mistakes get made; nuances get lost. Anyone who has ever produced a quantitative measure—whether a reject count in a factory or a publication count in a university—knows just how much distortion is possible, whether or not intentional.

All of this is not a plea for getting rid of hard information. That makes no more sense than getting rid of soft information. It means **we have to cease being mesmerized by the numbers and so stop letting the hard information drive out the soft.**

We all know about using hard facts to check out the soft hunches. Well, how about using soft hunches to check out the hard facts (e.g., "eyeballing" the statistics)? How about what we see with our own eyes and hear with our own ears? Such information may be idiosyncratic, but it can also be direct and rich, and so counter the disconnect that is all too common in executive suites today.

THE ENIGMA OF ORDER

Next come three conundrums on the people plane.

Organizations need order. Sometimes they need disorder, too—shaking up—but most of the time most organizations need to concentrate on the stable delivery of their goods and services.

And it is on their managers that the responsibility for ensuring much of this order falls: to provide the people in the unit with definition, predictability, a sense of what is and what can be, so that they can get on with their work of hiring people, planning operations, and producing outputs.

Here is where we find the traditional equating of the word *management* with *control*, much of it in the form of conventional strategies and structures—one to establish direction, the other to specify responsibilities.

Yet while seeking to impose such order, managers often find themselves functioning in a disorderly way. That was the message of Chapter 2. As Tom Peters put it, in managerial work "'sloppiness' is normal, probably inevitable, and usually sensible" (1979:171).

Why? **Because while every organization wants to keep going, some outside forces inevitably keep changing.** Inside, people may need predictability, but the outside world can have this nasty habit of being unpredictable. Customers change their minds; new technologies appear; unions call strikes. This is true even for something so orderly as organization structure itself: "Subordinates need to be given a clear understanding of their jobs and their boundaries, yet jobs inevitably overlap and boundaries are blurred" (Sayles 1979:4).

Someone has to deal with the unexpected, and often that is the manager him- or herself: the person whose responsibilities are broad enough and whose job is flexible enough to face the uncertainties and ambiguities.

So the Enigma of Order reads, **How to bring order to the work of others when the work of managing is itself so disorderly?** As Andy Grove of Intel put it: "Let chaos reign, then rein in chaos" (1995:141). The perfect conundrum!

Can disorderly activities produce orderly results? Of course they can. Think about artists, inventors, architects. Some of these people are about as disorderly as you can get, yet they can come up with the most orderly of results. And so, too, can it be the case with managers.

Contaminating the Order

Is what we have here really a conundrum, or just a curiosity? It would seem the latter, until we appreciate how a disorderly process can contaminate its orderly results, and vice versa.

Let's go back to the painters. No few of them display their personal disorder on their canvases—their inner turmoil, as in much of van Gogh's work, or Munch's "The Scream." Yet even these canvases can be surprisingly orderly. There is, of course, no shortage of disorderly art, but most of it is soon forgotten. In art, that may not much matter; in management, it does. What makes this a conundrum is how easily disorderly managing can render an organization disorderly too. Managers simply pass on their conflicts and ambiguities—they are the sieves discussed in Chapter 3. Of course, that can also happen in reverse: people in the unit can pass their disorder on to their manager.

So how are managers to deal with this conundrum? Like all the others: by nuancing its two sides. They have to weave back and forth between letting the chaos reign and reining in the chaos.

Giving in to either side wreaks havoc on a unit. Too much order and its work becomes rigid, detached. Too little order, and its people can't function. We all know managers who let the chaos of their jobs, and that of the outside world, flow into their unit, without providing the necessary buffering. And so too do we all know managers so protective of their unit that it becomes detached from reality. Everything seems so neat and orderly—until things blow up in everybody's face.

THE PARADOX OF CONTROL

The Enigma of Order is difficult enough. Pile one manager upon another in the hierarchy and you get the Paradox of Control. Order is imposed by the manager above ("Increase production by 30 percent," etc.), except that below is a manager, too, working in his or her own disorder, with pressures from customers, communities, economies. As a consequence, the Enigma of Order becomes the Paradox of Control: **How is a manager to maintain the necessary state of controlled disorder when the manager above is imposing order?**

The Damage from Deeming

Here is where management by deeming can become especially destructive. It is certainly convenient for senior managers to deem: sweeping ambiguity under the rug by imposing specific performance standards on their reports. "You need some sense of direction from me? Good. Here it is. The targets are clear. Meet them!"

But what do these targets constitute—where did the numbers come from? As we all know, they can sometimes be arbitrary, and even contradictory, picked out of the thin air of wish lists, with little regard for the difficult situations in which they have to be met. An awful lot of the ambiguity associated with such targets gets swept, not just under the rug, but into the faces of more junior managers. **So a good deal of deeming, which is becoming increasingly prevalent in large organizations, amounts to an executive cop-out.**

Compounding This Conundrum

Compared with other managers, chief executives have somewhat free rein. Boards may be demanding, but usually not so much as CEOs themselves. They face the Enigma of Order; managers down the hierarchy face the Paradox of Control too.

As the pressures for order descend the hierarchy, as managers "prove to their bosses that they are loyal and responsible by transmitting a goodly percentage of the demands of upper management down to their subordinates" (Sayles 1979:115), the weight of these pressures increases, until finally the whole "cascade" falls on the managers at the bottom of the hierarchy. Yet these are the ones least able to hide, for they usually have to face the disgruntled customers, the angry workers, the strident activists.

It is the senior managers who can often hide—in their systems, namely, their abstractions. They can pretend that all that planning and controlling will take care of the ambiguities. It does, at least at their level, and for a time. President Truman was famous for a plaque on his desk that read "The buck stops here." All too often these days it is the opposite: deeming managers pass the buck down, level by level, until it stops where the rubber hits the road.

So what are the pressured managers at lower levels to do? Morris et al. suggest that sometimes they can ignore the chain of command, at least when they have the "wisdom of knowing where and how to disobey" orders. "Sophisticated" managers develop this "into an art form" (1981:143). Moreover (as discussed in the posture of Managing Out of the Middle in the last chapter), they can turn the tables and promote change up the hierarchy. And managers at more senior levels can help by appreciating the consequences of passing down problems that are essentially theirs to resolve.

THE CLUTCH OF CONFIDENCE

Our last people conundrum is easier to explain if no less difficult to handle.

It takes a good deal of confidence to practice management effectively. Think about all the pressures, not to mention all these conundrums. As was evident in so much of the managing I observed (in the refugee camps, the NHS, Greenpeace, etc.), this is no work for the faint-hearted or the insecure. Any manager inclined to avoid problems, pass them on, or simply cover their own rear ends can make life dreadful for everyone else.

But how about the managers who are supremely confident? They can be even worse. Bear in mind the shaky foundations on which such confidence can lie: information about which one can never be sure; issues loaded with ambiguities; conundrums that cannot be resolved, often forcing managers to "wing it."

All alone, the managers have to convey the impression that they know where they are going, even when they are not sure, so that others feel safe to follow. In other words, managers often have to feign confidence. For modest managers, this can be difficult enough; for the supremely confident, it may be not difficult at all, just catastrophic.

The trouble with even reasonable confidence is that it can carry the manager over the edge, and down a slippery slope—to arrogance. It does not take much for someone in this job to stop listening, become isolated, think of him- or herself as heroic.

The edge between confidence and arrogance can be not only thin but also vague. A manager can cross it without being aware. And once on the way down that slope, there may be no stopping, until reaching the bottom. So the Clutch of Confidence reads, **How to maintain a sufficient level of confidence without crossing over into arrogance?**

This is not a casual conundrum. It probably undermines as much management practice, and causes as much grief for other people, as any of the other conundrums. This is especially true in this age of heroic leadership, where even modest managers, when successful, can get put on pedestals for all to revere.

In Praise of the Modest Manager

How can a manager avoid this Clutch of Confidence? Honest friends and advisers can help. When someone is going over that edge, as every successful person does from time to time, it is helpful to have someone to yank him or her back. But, of course, having such friends and advisers—and listening to them—requires a certain amount of confidence too, at least inner confidence, which, happily, is usually accompanied by a certain modesty. So **perhaps the key to dealing with this conundrum is to ensure that more people who are confidentially modest end up in management positions in the first place.** But these days the opposite has become too common, in two ways: modest people get precluded and arrogant ones selected.

THE AMBIGUITY OF ACTING

The next two conundrums happen on the action plane.

If managing is about making sure that things get done, then managers have to be decisive. They cannot hedge too much, and they can be reflective only to a point. Managers have to take stands, making decisions and provoking actions that move their units forward.

The problem is that much of this has to be done under difficult circumstances, full of ambiguities. And this gives rise to another conundrum: **How to act decisively in a complicated, nuanced world?**

The Doubtfulness of Decision

Consider *decision* itself. The very term seems decisive. Decisions are, after all, commitments to action. But need we always commit—that is, decide—in order to act? If you believe so, have someone hit you on the knee. Or visit a courtroom and listen to a second-degree murder case—that is action without decision. Organizations sometimes get tapped on the knee, too. There was a story some years ago about the senior management of a major European automobile company hiring consultants to find out how a new model came to be.

When we do make a commitment—that decision to act—is it necessarily as clear as it appears? And just because we commit, does that mean we act? A lot can happen between deciding and doing. "Many decisions must be reconsidered and remade" (Sayles 1979:11).

Confidence enables a manager to act decisively, yet being too decisive in the face of ambiguity can amount to arrogance—especially when the manager is distant from the issue in question. Consider all those ill-conceived acquisitions in large corporations, when bold decisions were taken in remarkable ignorance of their consequences. Or how about George W. Bush's 2003 decision to go to war in Iraq?

Conversely, managers who hesitate to act can bring everything to a halt. Some sort of decision may be better than no decision at all—at least it gets people moving. But managers who act too quickly, even when well informed, may be forcing their organizations into premature action on events that are still unfolding.

Of course, events are always unfolding. And major events usually unfold unpredictably. So **the trick is to know when to wait, despite the costs of delay, and when to act, despite unforeseeable consequences.** And for that there is no manual, no course, not even any five easy steps—just informed judgment.

Back to Chunking

If many decisions have to be remade anyway, why not "chunk" them into successive steps, with time for feedback in between?

Chapter 2 introduced the metaphor of juggling, about the many projects and issues that a manager has to handle concurrently. He or she has to integrate on the run: as an issue comes down, it has to be given a new burst of energy, while all the other issues keep spinning in midair.

Charles Lindblom labeled such behavior "disjointed incrementalism," describing it as "typically a never ending process of successive steps in which continual nibbling is a substitute for a good bite" (1968:25–26). He referred to "the piecemeal remedial incrementalist" as perhaps not looking "like a heroic figure" but someone who "is, nevertheless, a shrewd, resourceful problem-solver who is wrestling broadly with a universe that he is wise enough to know is too big for him" (p. 27).

THE RIDDLE OF CHANGE

As noted in Chapter 1, these days we hear a great deal of hype about change,. Yet our automobile engines use the same technology as the Ford Model T. Even the claims about change haven't changed:

> Few phenomena are more remarkable yet few have been less re-marked than the degree in which material civilization, the progress of mankind in all those contrivances which oil the wheels and promote the comforts of daily life have been concentrated in the last half century. It is not too much to say that in these respects more has been done, richer and more prolific discoveries have been made, grander achievements have been realized in the course of the 50 years of our own lifetime than in all the previous lifetimes of the race.

This appeared in *Scientific American*—in 1868!

My point in Chapter 1 was that we only notice what is changing, not what isn't, which includes most of what is around us. We also hear plenty about the problems of people resisting change in organizations. What we need to hear more about is all the change that is dysfunctional.

No manager can manage change alone—that is anarchy. Every manager has to manage continuity as well, which gives us the

Riddle of Change: **How to manage change when there is the need to maintain continuity?** Once again, the trick is to get the balance right.

Chester Barnard was quoted earlier noting that "executive work is not that of the organization, but the specialized work of maintaining the organization in operation" (1938:215). This means keeping the organization on track and getting it back on track when it goes off, as well as improving the track when necessary, and sometimes building new track to a different place.

My colleague Jonathan Gosling interviewed a number of managers about how they managed change. To his surprise, mostly they talked about managing continuity. Likewise, during the twenty-nine days I saw much change that was intertwined with continuity. Abbas Gullet and Stephen Omollo in the Red Cross refugee camps were promoting changes, to ensure stability, while John Cleghorn of the Royal Bank was championing changes small and large—fixing a sign, acquiring an insurance company—to keep the big bank on its course.

The Dual Search for Certainty and Flexibility

In an insightful book entitled *Organizations in Action,* James D. Thompson wrote about this conundrum as "the paradox of administration"—"the dual search for certainty and flexibility." Mostly he described how organizations function for the "reduction of uncertainty and its conversion into relative certainty" to protect their basic operations. Yet "the central characteristic of the administrative process [is a] search for flexibility" (1967:148).

Thompson believed that this paradox could be addressed by favoring certainty in the short run—for operating efficiency—and flexibility in the long run—for "freedom from commitment" (p. 150). The problem, of course, is that the long run never arrives (or, at least, as John Maynard Keynes put it, we are all dead by then). So managers have to face this conundrum, like all the others, in the short run—namely, in their current behavior.

As already suggested, there is always some change amid the continuity, even if hidden in some skunkworks. And there is always some continuity—some pockets of stability—amid the change. Organizations can experience some periods where change is pervasive, and other periods of relative stability. As in the Bible, for organizations too, there is a time to sow and a time to reap.

THE ULTIMATE CONUNDRUM

We can conclude with two general conundrums. The first: **How can any manager possibly manage all these conundrums concurrently?**

These are not convenient phenomena that appear on schedule or happily spaced apart. They are all mixed up with managing. So **to manage is not just to walk a tightrope but to move through a multidimensional space on all kinds of tightropes.**

I have noted a few times that the trick is to get the balance right. This, however, is not a stable balance but rather a dynamic one. Conditions cause managers to go one way much of the time (e.g., toward greater confidence when challenged, or toward more change when faced with opportunity) and later back the other way.

I have also noted repeatedly that such conundrums are unresolvable. As Charles Handy put it: "Paradoxes are like the weather, something to be lived with . . . the worst aspects mitigated, the best enjoyed and used as clues to the way forward" (1994:12-1).

There are no solutions because each conundrum has to be dealt with in context. **These paradoxes, predicaments, labyrinths, riddles, and others are built into managerial work—they *are* managing—and there they shall remain. To repeat a key point, they can be alleviated but never eliminated, reconciled but never resolved.** So managers have to face them, understand them, reflect on them, play with them. As F. Scott Fitzgerald wrote, "The test of a first-rate intelligence is the ability to hold two opposed ideas in the mind at the same time and still retain the ability to function." Can we afford any other form of intelligence in the world of managing?

Of course, all of this means that the manager's ultimate conundrum—how to deal with all these conundrums concurrently—remains. Maybe, then, the only hope lies in the final conundrum, my own.

MY CONUNDRUM

How do I reconcile the fact that, while all these conundrums can be stated apart, they all seem to be the same? I have offered plenty of comments about the overlapping of these conundrums, the similarities among them, even ones that seem to restate others. Maybe they are all just one big jumbled management conundrum. In that case, as a manager, you needn't be bothered by the previous, ultimate conundrum—just all the ones that preceded it.

6 Managing Effectively

Getting to the essence of managing

Trying to figure out what makes a manager effective, even *whether* a manager has been effective, is difficult. Believing in easy answers only makes it harder. Managers, and those who work with them, have to face the complexities. Helping to do so is the purpose of this chapter.

We begin with the supposedly effective but in fact inevitably flawed manager. This leads us into a brief discussion of unhappily managed organizational families, which we compare with happily managed ones. We turn then to the questions of selecting, assessing, and developing effective managers, asking along the way, "Where has all the judgment gone?" Woven throughout are many of the main points developed in this book, to serve as a kind of summary. This chapter, and book, close with a comment on "managing naturally."

THE MANY QUALITIES OF THE SUPPOSEDLY EFFECTIVE MANAGER

Lists of the qualities of effective managers abound. These are usually short—who would take dozens of items seriously? For example, in a brochure (circa 2005) to promote its EMBA program, entitled "What Makes a Leader?" the Rotman School of Management at the University of Toronto answered, "The courage to challenge the status quo. To flourish in a demanding environment. To collaborate for the greater good. To set clear direction in a rapidly changing world. To be fearlessly decisive."

But this list is clearly incomplete. Where is possessing native intelligence, or being a good listener, or just plain having energy? Fear not—they appear on other lists. So if we are to trust any of these lists, we shall have to combine all of them.

This, for the sake of a better world, I have done in Figure 12. It lists the qualities from various lists that I have found, plus a few missing favorites of my own. This composite list contains fifty-two items. Be all fifty-two and you are bound to be an effective manager. Even if not a human one.

THE INEVITABLY FLAWED MANAGER

All of this is part of that "romance of leadership" mentioned earlier (Meindl et al. 1985), which puts ordinary mortals on pedestals ("Rudolph is the perfect person for the job—he will save us!") so that we can vilify them as they come crashing down ("How could Rudolph have failed us so?"). Yet some managers do stay up, if not on that silly pedestal. How so?

FIGURE 12   **Composite List of Basic Qualities for Assured Managerial Success**

courageous	charismatic
committed	passionate
curious	*inspiring*
confident	visionary
candid	energetic/enthusiastic
reflective	upbeat/optimistic
insightful	ambitious
open-minded/tolerant (of people, ambiguities, and ideas)	tenacious/persistent/zealous
innovative	collaborative/participative/ cooperative
communicative (including being a good listener)	*engaging*
connected/informed	supportive/sympathetic/ empathetic
perceptive	stable
thoughtful/intelligent/*wise*	dependable
analytic/objective	fair
pragmatic	accountable
decisive (action-oriented)	ethical/honest
proactive	consistent
	flexible
	balanced
	integrative
	tall*

Source: Compiled from various sources; *my own favorites in italics.*

*This item appeared on no list that I saw. But it might rank ahead of many of the other items because studies have shown that managers are on average taller than other people. To quote from a 1920 study, entitled *The Executive and His Control of Men,* based on research done a lot more carefully than much of what we find in the great journals of today, Enoch Burton Gowin addressed the question "Viewing it as a chemical machine, is a larger body able to supply a greater amount of energy?" More specifically, might there be "some connection between an executive's physique, as measured by height and weight, and the importance of the position he holds?" (1920:22, 31). The answer, in statistic after statistic gathered by the author, is yes. Bishops, for example, averaged greater height than the preachers of small towns; superintendents of school systems were taller than principals of schools. Other data on railroad executives, governors, etc., supported these findings. The "Super-intendents of Street Cleaning" were actually the second tallest of all, after the "Reformers." (The "Socialist Organizers" were just behind the "police chiefs" but well up there.) Musicians were at the bottom of the list (p. 25).

The answer is simple: **Successful managers are flawed—we are all flawed—but their particular flaws are not fatal under the circumstances.** (Superman was flawed, too—remember Kryptonite?) Peter Drucker commented at a conference that "the task of leadership is to create an alignment of strengths, so as to make people's weaknesses irrelevant." He might have added "including the leader's own."

If you want to uncover someone's flaws, marry them or else work for them. Their flaws will quickly become apparent. So will something else (at least if you are a mature human being who has made a reasonable choice): that you can usually live with these flaws. Managers and marriages do succeed. The world, as a consequence, continues to unfold in its inimitably imperfect way.[7]

Fatally flawed are those superman lists of managerial qualities, because they are utopian. Some of the time they are just plain wrong. For example, managers should be decisive—who can argue with that? For starters, anyone who followed the machinations of George W. Bush, who learned the importance of being decisive from case studies in a Harvard classroom. The University of Toronto list calls this quality "fearlessly decisive." Going into Iraq, President Bush was certainly that. As for some of the other items on that list, this president's arch enemy in Afghanistan certainly "had the courage to challenge the status quo," while Ingvar Kamprad, who built IKEA into one of the most successful

---

[7] Not always. Politicians concentrate on hiding their flaws during election campaigns until they become fatal in office. For example, the object of the political debates on television is to demonstrate that your opponent is flawed while you are not. The assumption is that the flawed candidate should lose. Perhaps this theatrical farce is one reason why people are so fed up with political leadership.

retail chains ever, (as noted) apparently took fifteen years to "set clear direction in a rapidly changing world." (Actually, he succeeded because the furniture world was not changing rapidly; he changed it.) So perhaps we need to proceed differently.

UNHAPPILY MANAGED ORGANIZATIONAL FAMILIES

Tolstoy began his novel *Anna Karenina* with the immortal words "Happy families are all alike; each unhappy family is unhappy in its own particular way." And so it may be with managers and their organizational families: they may have an unlimited number of ways to screw up, with ever more fascinating ones being invented every day,[8] but perhaps only a few by which to succeed.

A Tale of Two Managers

Let me bring two managers into the picture. Liz and Larry were smart, well-educated, modern managers. They worked near each other in the same company, one heading a major staff group, the other a major line operation. Liz leapt; Larry lingered. One made decisions too quickly, so that they often had to be remade; the

---

[8] I was told the story of the chief executive of a major British company who would not let regular employees walk past the door of his office. To get by, they had to go down one set of stairs and up another. Those who got into that office had to sit on chairs lower than his, so that he could talk down to them. He moved to the chairmanship of an even greater company, and eventually he got knighted for his efforts. When he left that chairmanship, his advice to his successor, at board meetings, was to (1) dress properly, (2) not smoke, and (3) keep control with a clear agenda. His successor, at his first board meeting, took off his jacket, lit a cigar, and asked, "What would you like to talk about?"

other had difficulty making decisions at all, or else made them in ambiguous ways. The results were similar: people in their units felt excluded, confused, discouraged.

Beyond their own units, into the rest of the organization, Liz confronted while Larry connived. She often fought with her colleagues in the company—she knew better than they did—except for the CEO, to whom she was deferential. Larry, in contrast, was careful not to upset anyone, so he hesitated to challenge anyone, even when necessary.

Each, by the way, would probably recognize the other in this description. But would they recognize themselves? I need to add that although their respective managerial families were not particularly happy, these managers were not failures. None of these flaws was fatal. Things got done. They just could have been done more effectively—and happily.

To be true to Tolstoy, I am not going to propose a definitive list of the causes of managerial failures. This book needn't be that long. If you wish to have such a list, let me suggest you go back to Figure 12 and reverse all the qualities there. For example, in place of *decisive*, put *waffling*; and in place of *upbeat*, *downbeat*. Or else consider overdoing each. For *decisive*, you can put *hasty*; for *upbeat*, *hyper*. Indeed, leave these qualities exactly as they are—just apply them in the wrong context. Be decisive without understanding the situation (that war in Iraq) or be upbeat in managing a funeral home.

What I offer here are some general categories of failure, labeled person failures, job failures, fit failures, and success failures. These are discussed briefly, so that we can spend more time on success

Person Failures

First are the failures that managers achieve by themselves. Some people just shouldn't be managers—for example, the reluctant ones, who don't relish the pace and the pressures. Perhaps they should work alone or in peer groups without responsibility for others.

Other people like the job but are not competent at it: for example, they are thoughtless or dislike people. These failures are surprisingly common, even among managers who have made it to senior positions. In a *Fortune* magazine article on "Why CEOs Fail," Charam and Colvin offered two prime answers: "bad execution" and "people problems." They commented on the former:

> Keeping track of all critical assignments, following up on them, evaluating them—isn't that kind of . . . boring? We may as well say it: Yes. It's boring. It's a grind. At least, plenty of really intelligent, accomplished, failed CEOs have found it so and you can't blame them. They just shouldn't have been CEOs. (1999:36)

This sounds like the macroleading discussed earlier. It is on the increase: managers who race down the "fast track" with the "quick fix." (You can tell them by their use of such language.) As CEOs in large corporations, they are inclined to merge, restructure, and downsize—all very fashionable, and often a lot easier than resolving complicated problems. Here is the Syndrome of Superficiality out of control.

These and other managers are imbalanced in their practice. As noted in Chapter 3, too much leading can favor style over substance, while too much thinking can cause the job to implode. Likewise, in Chapter 4 we discussed an overemphasis on the art, craft, or science of managing, leading to styles that were labeled narcissistic, tedious, and calculating

Many of the common imbalances of managing can also be seen in the conundrums. As noted in Chapter 5, a sure way to fail is to resolve any of these conundrums, for example the Riddle of Change by promoting too much change or too little. Similarly, with regard to the characteristics of managing discussed in Chapter 2, too hectic a pace, too much fragmentation, or an excess of oral communication can send the job over the edge—as seems to be happening with increasing frequency these days, thanks to not using that off button.

All of this is not to make the case for perfect balance in managing. That can also be a form of imbalance, with the manager exhibiting no focus, no character, no style of his or her own.

Job Failures

Sometimes a person is well suited to managing and well balanced in his or her approach, but the job is simply not doable. It is literally unmanageable, and so the person fails. In the last chapter, for example, we noted unnatural managerial jobs—ones that should not exist.

A manager can also fail because the job is embedded in an organization or an outside context that makes it impossible. Think of the officer in charge of rearranging the deck chairs on the *Titanic* or the Vice President of Anything at Enron as it went down. How about being the sales manager of a company with shoddy, unsellable products? Don't blame the manager, except for taking the job.

Fit Failures

Next are the competent, balanced managers in doable jobs, just not the jobs for them. So they become unbalanced and therefore incompetent—misfits quite literally.

Here, again, the stories are legion, some of them stemming from the fallacy of professional management—that any properly trained manager can manage anything. I recall a business school that named a dean who had been running a trucking company. He claimed that managing professors was just like managing truck drivers. So most of the competent truck driver/professors left.

There is also the Peter Principle, about managers rising to their level of incompetence (Peter and Hull 1969). They should have been promoted once less often. Managerial experience at one level in a hierarchy does not necessarily suit managing at a more senior level. And vice versa: try putting a CEO into an operating position. He or she may be too used to being surrounded by people who look after the details.

Fit can also become misfit when conditions change, so that positive qualities turn into serious flaws. For example, an organization in crisis may find itself being managed by someone more suitable to managing in steady state. Or a turnaround artist is brought into an organization that is running perfectly well, so what ain't broke thus gets fixed. How about army officers trained for conventional warfare who find themselves facing guerrillas?

But be careful here: evident matches can prove to be mismatches, too. Sometimes matches of opposites work better than matches of likes—what we might call intentional misfits. Does a machine organization need a highly cerebral chief? Maybe it needs one who can open up its narrow tendencies, just as a wild and woolly adhocracy can sometimes benefit from an organized chief, to keep a lid on the madness.

Success Failures

Finally are the failures that derive from success. A company grows too large for its founding entrepreneur, or hubris sets into the management of a research establishment that has done very well. In an intriguing book called *The Icarus Paradox*,[9] which could have also been titled *The Perils of Excellence*, Danny Miller (1990) demonstrated how the strength of an organization can turn into weakness, so that its success becomes a failure. For example, "growth-driven, entrepreneurial builders . . . managed by imaginative leaders . . . [become] impulsive, greedy imperialists, who . . . [expand] helter-skelter into businesses they know nothing about" (p. 6). In other cases, the doers become overdoers; the linkers become gadflies; the leaders become cheerleaders. And established managers who take themselves too seriously—or CEOs who attribute the inherited success of their organization to themselves—slip over the edge of confidence, into arrogance. Yet many of these are allowed to soldier on, despite the misery of their managing.

To conclude, many pitfalls accompany the practice of managing. Someone once defined an expert as someone who avoids all the many pitfalls on his or her way to the grand fallacy. Managers, too, not just experts.

---

[9] The book was named for the figure in Greek mythology who flew so high that the sun melted his wings and sent him tumbling to his death.

HAPPILY MANAGED ORGANIZATIONAL FAMILIES

OK, enough about failure. We can dwell on that forever. What matters is success. And there is no shortage of that, more or less. As the story of Liz and Larry suggests, flawed managers can perform well enough. They succumb to some of the pitfalls without finding their way to the grand fallacy. In fact, many of the twenty-nine managers of my study were more than good enough: they created or sustained happy organizational families. How did they do that?

Wouldn't it be nice if I could offer the answer in five easy steps? I can't, but I can offer a framework to consider it.

Lewis et al., in the introduction to their book *No Single Thread: Psychological Health in Family Systems*, commented, "There is considerable literature on the pathological family types, but a 'scarcity of data' on the healthy family" (1976:xvii). What do we really understand about healthy organizations?

A Framework for Effectiveness

What I offer here is no formula, no theory, not even a set of propositions, just a framework (not a list) by which to think about managerial effectiveness in context. As shown in Figure 13, at the center are five "threads," or "managerial mindsets," as we call them in our International Masters in Practicing Management (see Gosling and Mintzberg 2003). They range from the more personal to the more social—labeled reflective, analytic, worldly, collaborative, and proactive. Two additional threads are shown at each end: being personally energetic and socially integrative.

FIGURE 13   **A Framework to Consider Managerial Effectiveness in Context**

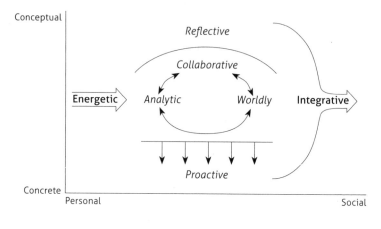

These threads are rooted in the practice of managing, as described in the roles in Chapter 3, more than in the nature of the person practicing those roles. Each thread is discussed in turn, then all of them are discussed together in conclusion. This section brings together many of the key points that have come out in this book.

When I read the Lewis et al. book on healthy families, I was struck by its parallels with the framework presented here (which I had already sketched out, although I subsequently borrowed the word *thread* from it). Indeed, I was able to find a quote from that book that matched each of these managerial threads, even one for how they have to be woven together: "We found no single quality that optimally functioning families demonstrated and that less fortunate families somehow missed. . . . Health at the level of family was not a single thread. . . . [C]ompetence must be considered as a tapestry" (1976:205–206).

The Energetic Thread

"Although [effective] families differ in the degree of energy displayed, they all demonstrated more constructive reaching out than did patently dysfunctional families" (Lewis et al. 1976:208–209). We can similarly expect a high degree of energy from effective managers, and from the units they manage, as well as a good deal of "reaching out." **If one thing is evident about the pace and the action of managing, it is the enormous amount of energy that effective managers bring to their work.** This is no job for the lazy.

Energy is largely a personal thread in this tapestry (or perhaps it is the loom), anchoring it on the left side of Figure 13. Of course, nothing in management is ever wholly personal. As Peter Brook, legendary director of the Royal Shakespeare Company, wrote in his book *The Empty Space* (1968), the audience energizes the actor as much as the actor energizes the audience.

This thread may help us understand how managers deal with two of the conundrums. The Quandary of Connecting asks how managers can keep informed when they are fundamentally removed, while the Riddle of Change asks how they can drive change while maintaining stability. This kind of energy is necessary to connect, to change, and to maintain stability.

The Reflective Thread

"In approaching problems within the family, [the healthy ones] explored numerous options; if one approach did not work, they backed off and tried another. This was in contrast to many dysfunctional families in which a dogged perseverance with a single approach was noted" (Lewis et al. 1976:208). My own observations suggest that **effective managers tend to be reflective: they know how to learn from their own experience; they explore numerous options; and they back off when one doesn't work, to try another.** This suggests a certain humbleness, not only about what the managers know, but also an appreciation of what they don't know.

As I noted in my book *Managers Not MBAs*, reflecting means "wondering, probing, analyzing, synthesizing, connecting—'to ponder carefully and persistently [the] meaning [of an experience] to the self'" (2004: 254, quoting Daudelin 1996:41). This goes beyond sheer intelligence, to a deeper wisdom that enables managers to be insightful—to see inside issues, beyond the obvious perceptions. As noted earlier, **the effective manager thinks and sees for him- or herself.**

If managing is hectic, then managers need to step back and reflect quietly on their own experience. Indeed, this can be an antidote for a number of the conundrums: the Clutch of Confidence, the Predicament of Planning, the Syndrome of Superficiality, the Quandary of Connecting. Figure 14 offers a set of self-study questions for managers. Some may seem simple, even rhetorical, but they can help to stimulate reflection.

FIGURE 14   **Self-Study Questions for Managers**

1. Where do I get my information, and how? Can I make greater use of my contacts? How can I get others to provide me with the information I need? Do I have sufficiently powerful mental models of those things I must understand?
2. What information do I disseminate? How can I get more information to others so they can make better decisions?
3. Do I tend to act before enough information is in? Or do I wait so long for all the information that opportunities pass me by?
4. What pace of change am I asking my unit to tolerate? Is this balanced with the needed stability?
5. Am I sufficiently well informed to pass judgment on the proposals submitted to me? Can I leave final authorization for more of these proposals to others?
6. What are my intentions for my unit? Should I make them more explicit to guide better the decisions of others? Or do I need flexibility to change them at will?
7. Am I sufficiently sensitive to the influence of my actions, and my managerial style in general? Do I find an appropriate balance between encouragement and pressure? Do I stifle initiative?
8. Do I spend too much time, or too little, maintaining my external relationships? Are there certain people whom I should get to know better?
9. In scheduling, am I just reacting to the pressures of the moment? Do I find the appropriate mix of activities, or do I overconcentrate on what I find interesting? Am I more efficient with particular kinds of work at special times of the day or week?
10. Do I overwork? What effect does my workload have on my efficiency and my family? Should I force myself to take breaks or reduce the pace of my activity?
11. Am I too superficial in what I do? Can I really shift moods as quickly and frequently as my schedule requires? Should I decrease the amount of fragmentation and interruption?
12. Am I a slave to the action and excitement of my job, so that I am no longer able to concentrate on issues? Should I spend more time reading and probing deeply into certain issues?
13. Do I use the different media appropriately? Do I know how to make the most of written communication and e-mail? Am I a prisoner of the pace of e-mail?
14. Do I rely excessively on face-to-face communication, thereby putting all but a few of my reports at an informational disadvantage? Do I spend enough time observing activities firsthand?
15. Do my obligations consume all my time? How can I free myself from them to ensure that I am taking the unit where I want it to go? How can I turn my obligations to my advantage?

Source: Adapted from Mintzberg (1973:175–177).

The Analytic Thread

As noted earlier, too much attention to analysis can be dysfunctional in the manager's job, but so, too, can too little, leading to a disorganized style of managing.

Looking for the key to effective managing in the light of analysis may be misguided, but expecting to find it in the obscurity of intuition is no more sensible. Once again, what makes sense is a certain balance: **the manager has to know formally and explicitly as well as informally and tacitly.** That is why the terms introduced at the end of Chapter 2, "calculated chaos" and "controlled disorder," apply so well to managerial work. In much the same way, Lewis et al. described the most dysfunctional families as presenting "chaotic structures" and the midrange families "rigid structures," while the "most competent families presented flexible structures" (p. 209).

The danger of overreliance on analysis came out especially in two of the conundrums: the Labyrinth of Decomposition, where so much around the manager is chopped into nice, neat, artificial categories; and the Mysteries of Measuring, where managers have to deal with that soft underbelly of hard data. But the Enigma of Order reminds us that the manager has to bring order out of the chaos of his or her work.

Skinner and Sasser (1997), in a *Harvard Business Review* article, may have had good reason to claim that effective managers "employ the practice of analysis with great effect" and "use analytic tools with . . . discipline and consistency." But when they concluded that effective managers are "above all else analyzers" (pp. 143, 148), in my opinion they were just plain wrong. An overemphasis on analysis in managing has driven out too much necessary judgment in organizations.

The Worldly Thread

"There is another complex family variable that involves respect for one's own world view as well as that of others" (Lewis et al. 1976:207).

We hear a great deal these days about managers having to be *global*; it is far more important that they be *worldly*. To be global implies a certain homogeneity and conformity. Is this what we want from our managers? It seems to me that we have too much of it already.

To think for themselves, managers require worldliness. ***Worldly* is identified in the *Pocket Oxford Dictionary* as "experienced in life, sophisticated, practical."** An interesting mixture of words! And perhaps as close as a set of words can get to what many of us want from our managers as true leaders.

To be worldly means to get into the worlds of other people—other cultures, other organizations, even other functions in one's own organization. To paraphrase lines by T. S. Eliot that have been overused for good reason, managers should be exploring ceaselessly in order to return to where they started and know the place for the first time. This is the worldly mindset.

"How can you possibly drive in this traffic?" asked an American manager of an Indian professor after she had arrived in Bangalore to attend the worldly mindset module of our IMPM program. "I just join the flow," he replied. Worldly learning had begun! There is a logic to other people's worlds that may seem disorderly to the outsider. Understand it and you will be a better manager—and more of a human being.

To appreciate other people's worlds does not mean to invade their privacy or "mind-read" them. Lewis et al. found these to be "destructive characteristics," seen only in "the most severely dysfunctional families" (p. 213). In the midrange families, they found pressures for conformity. But in the healthy families, these researchers found what they called "respectful negotiation":

> Because separateness with closeness was the family norm, differences were tolerated and conflicts were approached through negotiation, which respected the rights of others to feel, perceive, and respond differently. There was no tidal pull toward a family oneness that obliterates individual distinctions. (p. 211)

If analysis is close to science on our art-craft-science triangle, then worldliness is close to craft, rooted in tangible experience and tacit knowledge.

One theme that was evident in all the conundrums, especially the Ambiguity of Acting (how to act decisively in a complicated, nuanced world), is the need for managers to exhibit a sense of nuance. Worldly managers, who have come to know their own place for the first time because they have gained insight into other places, may be particularly effective in dealing with the conundrums.

The Collaborative Thread

"The trend toward an egalitarian marriage was in striking contrast to both the more distant (and disappointing) marriages of the adequate families and the marital pattern of dominance and submission that so often was seen in dysfunctional families" (Lewis et al. 1976:210).

As we move along our tapestry, the social aspects of managing become more prominent. Collaboration is not about "motivating" or "empowering" people—which, as noted earlier, may just reinforce the manager's authority—but about helping them to work together. Kaz Mishina, when he directed our IMPM module on the collaborative mindset in Japan, described this as "leadership in the background—letting as many ordinary people as possible lead."

In the "engaging" style of managing, introduced in Chapter 4 and described here in Figure 15, the manager engages him- or herself in order to engage others. There is a sense of respecting, trusting, caring, and inspiring, not to mention listening. To draw further from the Lewis et al. book, "Healthy families were open in the expression of affect. The prevailing mood was one of

FIGURE 15 **Engaging Management**

- Managers are important to the extent that they help other people to be important.
- An organization is an interacting network, not a vertical hierarchy. Effective managers work throughout; they do not sit on top.
- Out of this network emerge strategies as engaged people solve little problems that can grow into big strategies. Implementation, so-called, also feeds formulation.
- To manage is to help bring out the positive energy that exists naturally within people. Managing thus means engaging, based on judgment, rooted in context.
- Leadership here is a sacred trust earned from the respect of others.

warmth, and caring. There was a well developed capacity for empathy" (p. 214).

As discussed in Chapter 4 on "Managing Beyond the Manager," the past century has seen a steady shift from managing as control to managing as engagement. We hear increasingly about knowledge workers and contract work, networked and "learning" organizations, teams and task forces, joint ventures and alliances. Many "subordinates" have become colleagues, and many suppliers have become partners, with a corresponding shift in managerial styles from controlling to convincing, leading to linking, empowering to engaging.

Delegating becomes less of a dilemma when a manager naturally inclined to collaborate keeps people in the unit well informed. And connecting becomes less of a quandary when managers who collaborate get better connected and so become more informed.

To conclude, please appreciate that there is nothing magical about this thread, no great characteristic of leadership. Like the other threads, it is perfectly natural, much as is living in a family that functions well.

The Proactive Thread

"There was little that was passive about healthy families. The family as a unit demonstrated high levels of initiative in responding to input" (Lewis et al. 1976:208–209).

All managerial activity, as noted several times in our discussion and was shown in Figure 13, is sandwiched between reflection in the abstract and action on the ground—"refl'action," in that word coined by our IMPM participant. **Too much reflection**

and nothing gets done; too much action and things get done thoughtlessly. So here we consider action on the ground, which encompasses the managerial roles of doing and dealing.

I have saved this for last among the five mindsets because, while reflectiveness is largely personal, activeness is fundamentally social: there can be no managerial action without the involvement of other people. **Managing is a social process. Managers who try to go it alone typically end up overcontrolling—issuing orders and deeming performance in the hope that authority will ensure compliance. This may work sometimes, but it hardly taps human potential.**

I use the term *proactive* rather than *active* to indicate that this thread is about managers seizing the initiative—initiating action instead of just responding to what happens. As I noted earlier, effective managers grab whatever degrees of freedom they can and run vigorously with them. To quote Isaac Bashevis Singer in what could be the motto for the effective manager: "We have to believe in free will; we've got no choice."

Thus, **effective managers do not act like victims. They are "agents of change," not "targets of change"** (Hill 2003:xiii). They go with the flow (like that traffic in Bangalore) while they influence the flow.

The most evident conundrum here is the Ambiguity of Acting (how to act decisively in a complicated, nuanced world). Being worldly can help, as can being reflective, but being proactive is key. Note that effective change is not just driven from the "top" down—deliberate, decisive, dramatic—but also from the bottom up and the middle out—experimental, incremental, emergent.

Proactiveness can be a characteristic of managers at all levels in the hierarchy, as we saw especially in the day of Alan Whelan of BT. And don't forget the Riddle of Change. Effective managers may drive change, but they also have to maintain stability, which can require just as much proactiveness, as was evident in those Red Cross camps.

The Integrative Thread

Let me repeat what may be Lewis et al.'s most important conclusion: "health at the level of family was not a single thread . . . competence must be considered as a tapestry" (p. 206). **Managing is a tapestry woven of the threads of reflection, analysis, worldliness, collaboration, and proactiveness, all of it infused with personal energy and bonded by social integration.**

In looking "at the essentials of leadership," Mary Parker Follett designated "of the greatest importance . . . the ability to grasp the total situation. . . . Out of a welter of facts, experiences, desires, aims, the leader must find the unifying thread . . . see a whole, not a mere kaleidoscope of pieces," by appreciating "the evolving situation, the developing situation." In other words, managing means synthesizing on the run, by learning "the mastery of [the] moment" (1920:168, 169, 170).

Synthesizing requires mastering across the moments, too. **Managing is about achieving a dynamic balance across the information, people, and action planes, while reconciling the concurrent needs for art, craft, and science, all the while juggling many issues.**

The word *analysis* seems clear enough, but the word *synthesis* is obscure. What does it mean to achieve synthesis, and would we even know it if we attained it? **A key purpose of managing is to strive for synthesis, continuously, without ever reaching it, or even knowing how close it is.** As discussed in Chapter 5, effective managers not only work deductively, and cerebrally, from reflection to action—formulation to implementation, the conceptual to the concrete. They also work inductively, insightfully, from action to reflection, with so-called implementation feeding back to formulation, the concrete to the conceptual, as they learn from experience. Above all, they cycle back and forth between these two, through those moments of mastery.

Don't assume, however, that reflecting and acting are necessarily separate and sequential. Thinking is an intrinsic part of acting: **Managers certainly think in order to act, but they also act in order to think—to discover what works. And above all, they think *while* they act:** "managerial activities can be done more or less thinkingly" (Weick 1980:19). But not alone: harnessing the "collective mind" is one of the great challenges facing contemporary organizations—for example, in crafting their strategies and establishing their cultures.

SELECTING EFFECTIVE MANAGERS

How to select managers who will be effective, how to assess whether they are actually being effective, and how can they be developed for greater effectiveness? The findings of this book are used to consider each of these questions in turn.

The subject of selecting managers for effectiveness has already received considerable attention elsewhere; here, I would just like to add a few thoughts of my own.

Choosing the Devil You Know. The perfect manager has yet to be born. If everyone's flaws come out sooner or later, then sooner is better. So **managers should be selected for their flaws as much as for their qualities.** Instead, the inclination has been to focus on people's qualities, sometimes a single one that blinds the people doing the selecting to everything else. "Sally's a great networker" or "Joe's a visionary," especially if the failed predecessor was a lousy networker or devoid of strategic vision.

No one should ever be selected without making every reasonable and ethical effort to identify his or her flaws—the devil's in the candidate.Then these flaws should be judged carefully against the managerial job in question, to avoid surprises. Performance in a previous managerial job may not give a reliable indication of potential in the next one, but it can offer a window into that person's flaws. Hence the next point.

Voice to the Managed. Managing happens within the unit as well as beyond it. Yet it is usually people beyond the unit who select the manager, whether that be the board in the choice of a chief executive or senior managers in the choice of junior ones. The danger here is that it can be easier to impress outsiders, who have not had to live with the candidates on a daily basis, than insiders who have. Charm may be one criterion for selection, but hardly the main one. As a consequence, too many organizations end up with managers who "kiss up and kick down"—overconfident, smooth-talking individuals who have exhibited little real leadership.

If one simple prescription could improve monumentally the effectiveness of managing, it is giving voice in selection processes to those people who know the candidates best— namely, the ones who have been managed by them. I am not calling here for the election of managers, only for a balanced assessment by insiders and outsiders together. Indeed, this is common practice in hospitals, universities, and law offices.[10]

Considering an Outside Insider. There is a tendency in some quarters, at least for senior positions, to favor an outsider—the new broom that can sweep the organization clean. Unfortunately, that sweeping may end up being done by the devil the selection committee does not know, who in turn who may not be able to distinguish the real dirt. So the new broom can sweep out the heart and soul of the enterprise. **Perhaps selection committees need to give more attention to the devils they do know, because these people know the dirt in the organization.**

In fact, selection committees can sometimes choose someone who quit in disgust—an outside insider. Such a person knows the situation, voted with his or her feet against it, and so may be ideal to drive a turnaround—a new broom familiar with the

---

[10] There is one famous company, for decades the leader in its field, whose chief executive is elected by a closed vote of its senior managers. I have asked many groups of businesspeople, all of whom know this company, to guess which it is. Rarely does anyone get it. The answer is McKinsey & Company, whose executive director is elected to a three-year term by a vote of the senior partners. This seems to have worked well for McKinsey. Has any McKinsey consultant ever proposed it to a client?

old dirt. Moreover, there will be insiders who can assess this person's qualities and flaws.

ASSESSING MANAGERIAL EFFECTIVENESS

You are a manager; you want to know how you are doing. Other people around you may be even more intent on finding out how you are doing. There are lots of easy ways to assess this. Beware of them all. **The effectiveness of a manager can only be judged in context.** This sounds easy enough, until you take it apart, here in terms of seven subpropositions. (Bear with me—I'll explain at the end why we need so many.)

(1) **Managers are not effective; matches are effective.** There is no such thing as a good husband or a good wife, only a good couple. And so it is with managers and their units. There may be people who fail in all managerial jobs, but there are none who can succeed in all of them. Success depends on the match between the person and the context, at the time, for a time. Thus, **(2) there are no effective managers in general,** which also means **(3) there is no such thing as a professional manager**—someone who can manage anything.

Of course, managers and their units succeed and fail together. So **(4) to assess managerial effectiveness, you also have to assess the effectiveness of the unit.** And not only that: **(5) you have to assess the contribution the manager made to that effectiveness.**

Some units function well despite their managers, and others would function a lot worse if not for their managers. So beware of assuming that the manager is automatically responsible for any success or failure of the unit. History matters; culture matters; markets matter; weather matters. How many managers have succeeded simply by maneuvering themselves into favorable jobs, making sure they did not mess up, and then taking credit for the success?

To further complete matters, **(6) managerial effectiveness also has to be assessed for broader impact, beyond the unit and even the organization.** What about the manager who makes the unit more effective at the expense of the broader organization? Manufacturing kept its costs so low that sales could not sell the manufactured products.

How many organizations measure the performance of their units, and managers, with regard to their contribution to the whole? Remember that **a healthy organization is not a collection of detached human resources but a community of engaged human beings.**

Moreover, what is right for the unit and the organization might be wrong for the world around it. For example, bribing customers: Is that effective? Sure, if you want to see it that way. But what's the use of imploring managers to be socially responsible and then failing to assess their irresponsibly "effective" behavior?

Put together all these points, and you have to ask: How can anyone who needs to assess a manager possibly cope with all this? The answer here, too, is simple—in principle. **(7) Managerial effectiveness has to be judged and not just measured.**

We can certainly get measures of effectiveness for some of these things, especially unit performance in the short run. But how are we to measure the rest? Where is the composite measure that answers the magic question?

If you think that so many points to assess managerial effectiveness is excessive, then think about the excessiveness of the executive bonuses that have ignored most of them. These have relied on the simplest of measures, such as increase in stock price. **The effectiveness of a chief executive's impact has to be assessed in the long run, but since we don't know how to measure that, at least as attributable to a specific executive, then executive bonuses should be eliminated. Period.**

Where Has All the Judgment Gone? Remember judgment? It used to be a key to managing effectively, even if though hidden in the dark recesses of the human brain. And then along came measurement, in the dazzling light. It was a good idea, so long as it informed judgment. Too frequently, however, it replaced judgment. So, sure, **measure what you can, but be sure to judge the rest; don't be mesmerized by measurement.**

In 1981, the Business Roundtable, a group of the chief executives of many of America's most prestigious companies, issued their "Statement on Corporate Responsibility."

> The shareholder must receive a good return but the legitimate concerns of other constituencies (customers, employees, communities, suppliers and society at large) also must have the appropriate attention.... [Leading managers] believe that enlightened consideration ... will best serve the interest of [the] shareholders. (quoted in Mintzberg, Simons, and Basu 2002:71; since removed from www.businessroundtable.org)

In 1997, this Business Roundtable issued another statement, entitled "Statement of Corporate Governance." This one turned the other on its head, claiming that the paramount duty of management and boards of directors is to the corporations' stockholders. It explained:

> The notion that the board must somehow balance the interests of stockholders against the interests of other stakeholders fundamentally misconstrues the role of directors. It is, moreover, an unworkable notion because it would leave the board with no criteria for resolving conflicts between the interest of stockholders and of other stakeholders or among different groups of stakeholders. (quoted in the same article; also since removed from www.businessroundtable.org)

No criteria indeed—except judgment! Some time between 1981 and 1997, by their own account, this collection of America's most prominent CEOs lost their capacity for judgment. If you want to understand what has been underlying the economic crisis in America, here you have it, in a nutshell: the judgment of its so-called leaders. (See www.mintzberg.org/enterprise.)

I write books and develop programs for managers. People sometimes ask me for measures of performance for these programs (at the limit, and I kid you not, "How much will our share price rise if we send Joanne, etc., on your program?"). I resist the urge to say "43 cents." Instead, I reply as follows:

"Consider a book you read recently: can you quantify its costs?" Sure: so much money to purchase it, so many hours to read it. "Good. Now, please quantify the benefits. If you can do that—measure its impact on you—please let me know and I will do the same for our program." As a reader, you might be finding this book wonderful—4.9 on some 5-point scale or other—and never do anything with it. Or you may have hated every word—a score of 1.3 (why are you still reading?)—yet use an idea from it five years from now without remembering its source. You can stop reading books if you like, but can you get rid of management (and a lot more) just because of the difficulties of measuring its performance?

DEVELOPING MANAGERS EFFECTIVELY

Now, how should managers be developed? In 1996, a few of us set out to rethink the world of management education and development, in order to change how management is practiced—toward what is described in this book. We began in our own place, with "management" education in the business school.

The conventional MBA is just that: about business administration. It does a fine job of teaching the business functions, but not of developing the practice of management. Indeed, by giving the impression that students with little experience have learned management, let alone leadership, these programs have instead promoted hubris.

Our efforts have given rise to the International Masters in Practicing Management (IMPM.org), mentioned a number of times and described in the accompanying box alongside three other programs that it engendered. But first a summary of what lies behind these efforts.

1. *Managers, let alone leaders, cannot be created in a classroom.* Management is a practice that cannot be taught as a science or a profession; in fact, it cannot be taught at all. Some of the best managers/leaders have never spent a day in

an MBA classroom, while no shortage of the worst sat there obediently for a couple of years.[11]

2. *Managing is learned on the job, enhanced by a variety of experiences and challenges.* No one gets to practice surgery or accounting without prior training in a classroom. In management, it has to be the opposite. As we have seen, the job is too nuanced, intricate, and dynamic to be learned prior to practice. So the logical starting point is the job itself. The first managerial assignment can be key, because that is when managers "are perhaps most open to experiences and learning the basics" (Hill 2003: 288). Beyond that, the learning can be enhanced by a variety of challenging managerial assignments (McCall 1988; McCall et al. 1978).

3. *Development programs can help managers make meaning of their experience, by encouraging them to reflect on it personally and to share it with their colleagues.* The classroom is a wonderful place to enhance the comprehensions and competencies of people who are already practicing management, especially when it draws on their own natural experience. In an uninterrupted place, managers can sit in small groups and consider their experience in the light of insightful concepts.

---

[11] See *Managers, Not MBAs* (Mintzberg 2004:1–194), including the report of a study done by Joseph Lampel and me (pp. 114–119). We took from a book published by a long-term Harvard Business School insider (Ewing 1990) a list of nineteen of its superstar CEOs and tracked their performance over 13 years. Ten of these CEOs were outright failures (the company went bankrupt, the CEO was fired, a major merger backfired, etc.), and another four had questionable records at best. Just five of the nineteen seemed to do fine.

4. *Intrinsic to this development has to be the carrying of the learning back to the workplace, for impact on the organization.* A major problem with management development is that it usually happens in isolation. The manager is developed, perhaps even changed, only to return to an unchanged workplace. Management development has to include organization development, designed to drive change in the organization.

5. *Programs for managers need to be organized according to the nature of managing itself* —for example, in terms of managerial mindsets, not business functions. Marketing + finance + accounting, etc., does not = management. Moreover, a focus on the business functions overemphasizes analysis, which is but one of the mindsets of managing.

NATURAL DEVELOPMENT: FROM MANAGEMENT TO ORGANIZATION TO SOCIETY TO SELF

In the mid-1990s, we began to rethink the whole issue of management education, which led to a family of new programs, four of which are described here.

IMPM: Combining management education with management development. The International Masters in Practicing Management (www. impm.org) has been designed to shift business education to management education, and combine it with management development. The intention has been to help experienced managers *do* a better job in their own organization, not *get* a better job in another one.

Five modules of ten days each, around the world, address the mindsets: reflection (about managing self) in the north of England, analysis (about managing organizations) in Canada (Montreal), worldliness (about managing context) in India (Bangalore), collaboration (about managing relationships) in China (Beijing), and action (about managing change) in Brazil (Rio de Janeiro).

Sitting in small groups at round tables, the managers spend about half the time learning from each other, through the sharing of reflections on their own experience. Sometimes they engage in "competency sharing"—about how they have practiced certain competencies (such as networking), to raise consciousness about their practice. They also do "friendly consulting," to help each other think through their managerial problems, and undertake "managerial exchanges," pairing up to spend several days at each other's workplace. The managers are encouraged to create Impact teams of colleagues or reports back home, to diffuse their learning and pursue its consequences for changing their organization (see Mintzberg 2011a).

ALP: Combining managerial development with organization development. So-called Advanced Management Programs are often just short replicas of conventional MBA programs: they use many of the same cases and much of the same theory; they are organized around the business functions; and they seat managers in the same linear rows.

The *Advanced* Leadership Program (www.alp-impm.com) carries the IMPM further. Here companies buy tables instead of chairs; they send teams of six managers, charged with addressing a key issue in their company. In three modules of one week each, spread over six months, the teams focus on friendly consulting to work through one another's issues.

IMHL: Adding in social development. The International Masters for Health Leadership (www.imhl.info), modeled after the IMPM, is for practicing managers, most with clinical backgrounds, from all aspects of health care, around the world. This program also uses the friendly consulting, but carried into social development. Besides bringing in issues of concern to their work and their organizations, the managers have been reaching out to broader health care issues in their communities, and using the class as a think tank.

Coaching Ourselves: Bringing it all to self-development. These earlier initiatives were carried to their natural conclusion by the then director of engineering in a high-technology company who needed to develop his own managers but had no budget to do so. When he heard about what we were doing in these programs, he followed suit, on his own. His group met informally, at lunch, every two weeks or so, to reflect on their experience, using conceptual materials to stimulate their discussions. This continued for two years, while some of the members of the initial group established groups of their own. CoachingOurselves.com was created as a consequence, to enable groups of managers in other organizations to engage in such self-directed learning. They download various topics, such as "Dealing with the Pressures of Managing," and work on them in informal sessions of about ninety minutes each, to strengthen their teams and drive changes in their organizations. Some organizations are now using Coaching Ourselves throughout their middle management. (For more on these programs, see Mintzberg 2004, 2011a, 2011b, and 2012.)

Managing is not going to be taught to anyone—not by any professor nor by any expert in development. Managers have to learn primarily through their own efforts. This can be facilitated in a classroom, but the message of our own experience is that **there is nothing so powerful, or so natural, as engaged managers who are committed to developing themselves, their organizations, and their communities.**

MANAGING NATURALLY

If management development can become more natural, then why not managing itself?

Which Species Is Out of Control?

As human beings, we presumably began in caves or the like, from which bands of us, in communities, went out to hunt and gather. We were probably organized much as flying geese are still organized: the strongest member took the lead and then ceded it as another became stronger. This did not mean that leadership, charisma, engagement, management, and all the rest did not exist, only that they blended into social processes in a natural way. Luckily for them, they lacked the benefit of thousands of books glorifying all this, and so they just got on with it.

We do have that benefit, and so all too often we don't get on with it. Over the years we have become increasingly organized. First, I suppose, came group leaders, who hunted and fought the enemies best and in some cases turned around to intimidate their followers. Over the millennia, this evolved into chiefs, lords, pharaohs, caesars, emperors, kings, queens, shoguns, czars, maharajahs, sultans, viceroys, dictators, führers, prime ministers, and presidents, not to mention managers, directors, executives, bosses, oligarchs, CEOs, COOs, CFOs, and CLOs.

Shouldn't all these labels be telling us something—namely, that we are a species out of control? In the Banff National Park, Gord Irwin mentioned a "bear jam"—a traffic jam caused by a bear. When one ambles down to the highway, the tourists stop—some even get out of their cars to take pictures—and the truckers fume. In that park, they referred to "managing the natural setting." But surely this is an oxymoron: that setting managed itself just fine for millennia without our "management." Now it has "bear management plans"!

Think about what management and leadership have become in the settings that are "natural" to us. We have taken something straightforward and made it convoluted: by putting "leaders" on pedestals; by turning human beings into human resources; by controlling them through excessive measuring; by believing that management is a profession; by developing bear management plans while we human beings fight with each other over our self-assumed right to "manage" the natural world. Where is plain old management?

If we really want to understand what has happened to management, then we would do well to get down on the ground, where the elk graze in the towns and the truckers battle the tourists. Then maybe we can work "up" from there, to the abstractions of management that so mesmerize us—where people earn larger incomes ostensibly because their work is more important but perhaps really because they have to cope with that much more nonsense, no small measure of it imposed by their own formalized systems. Supposedly developed to deal with the complexities, perhaps all of this is really a conceptual smokescreen for a species out of control, alien to its own natural environment. After all, the bears know full well that the real problem is "people jams."

So How About Simply Managing?

So let's wake up to our humanity and get past our childish obsession with leadership. **What could be more natural than to treat**

our organizations, not as mystical hierarchies of authority, but as communities of engagement, where every member is respected and so returns that respect? Sure, we need people called managers to coordinate some efforts, provide some direction in complex social systems, and support the people who simply want to get their work done. But these managers have to work with such people, not rule over them.

Richard Boyatzis of Case Western Reserve University has written: "There appears to be no images, metaphors, or models for management from natural life," and so "management is an unnatural act" (1995:50). Sure, managing people is a lot more complicated than leading a pack of geese or emitting a chemical substance to hold together a beehive. But managing is a perfectly natural act that we make unnatural by disconnecting it from its natural context, and so not seeing it for what it is.

This suggests that we are wasting our time obsessing about great managers and leaders. Perhaps we should instead be appreciating that reasonably normal people, flawed but not fatally so in their contexts, can manage and lead rather successfully. To express this more forcefully: **To be a successful manager, let alone—dare I say—a great leader, maybe you don't have to be wonderful so much as more or less emotionally healthy and clearheaded:** clear about the myths of managing, clear enough to think for yourself, clear about your own limitations as well as the limitless potential of other people, clear about which way the world is headed and how that can be changed. That, at least, is what I saw in many of the twenty-nine days of managing that I observed.

Sure, there are narcissists and other dysfunctional types who succeed for a time. But show me one of these and I'll show you many others who failed miserably. The man who originally put management on the map said simply, "No institution can possibly survive if it needs geniuses or supermen to manage it. It must be organized in such a way as to be able to get along under a leadership composed of average human beings" (Drucker 1946:26).

How to get to such natural leadership? As Drucker suggested, we can start by stopping to build organizations that are dependent on heroic leadership. No wonder we can't get past this: when one hero fails, we search frantically for another. Meanwhile, the organization—school, hospital, government, business—flounders. **By the excessive promotion of leadership, we demote everyone else. We create clusters of followers who have to be driven to perform, instead of leveraging the natural propensity of people to cooperate in communities.** In this light, **effective managing can be seen as engaged to be engaging, connected to be connecting.**

I like to believe that the subject of this book strikes at the heart of our lives today—our increasingly "organized" lives. We need to rethink management and organization, beyond leadership to communityship, by realizing how simple, natural, and healthy they all can be.

Dedication

I dedicate this edition of *Simply Managing* to Berrett-Koehler, an engaging organization.

Steve Piersanti was the president of a highly successful division of a large publisher when, during a round of cost cutting, he was ordered to reduce his staff by 10 percent. He refused, arguing that his unit had been doing well and lacked the turnover that made such cutting easier for other units. When a number of authors and suppliers found out that he had been fired, they encouraged him to start his own company and offered to support it. Thus was Berrett-Koehler born.

And thus has it functioned ever since: this is a different kind of publisher. The staff hardly turns over: many of the same competent and dedicated people have been there for years. They believe in books beyond sales, causes beyond shareholder value, and authors' ideas beyond their reputations. "Creating a world that works for all" is not just the company's stated mission; it is reflected in the books it produces and how it functions internally. The consequence of this is perhaps best reflected in the fact that, when the company needed some funding and approached its authors, sixty of them bought shares in the enterprise.

Berrett-Koehler consults its authors on every aspect of their books, including design. In fact, it holds an Author Day for each one. The author comes into the offices in San Francisco and discusses the book with an enthusiastic staff of editors, designers, producers, marketers, foreign rights people, and others. It is quite a special day. The highlight is the Author Lunch, attended by the entire staff in the office that day as well as invited guests, during which he or she gets the chance to present the book. I renamed one of my books because of a comment made at that lunch by the representative of a chain of bookstores.

The name Piersanti & Company was dismissed at the outset. Instead, the two founders, Steve and his wife, searched their own genealogies. After considering various options, they decided on Berrett, the name of Steve's great-grandmother, and Koehler, that of his wife's grandfather.

Steve Piersanti is not a heroic leader; he is an engaged manager, quiet and modest, but most determined. He follows no crowds, and Berrett-Koehler has published books that established publishers would not touch.

I am proud to be an author and community owner of Berrett-Koehler Publishers, Inc.

References

A fuller bibliography of the research and other writing on this subject can be found in *Managing* (Mintzberg, 2009).

Alinsky, S. D. (1971). *Rules for Radicals: A Pragmatic Primer for Realistic Radicals.* New York: Random House.

Andrews, F. (1976). Management: How a Boss Works in Calculated Chaos. *New York Times,* October 29.

Augier, M. (2004). James March on Education, Leadership, and Don Quixote: Introduction and Interview. *Academy of Management Learning & Education*, 3(2), 169–177.

Barnard, C. I. (1938). *The Functions of the Executive.* Cambridge, MA: Harvard University Press.

Bennis, W. G. (1989). *On Becoming a Leader.* Reading, MA: Perseus Books.

Boyatzis, R. E. (1995). Cornerstones of Change: Building the Path for Self-Directed Learning. In R. E. Boyatzis, S. S. Cowen, & D. A. Kolb (Eds.), *Innovation in Professional Education: Steps on a Journey from Teaching to Learning* (pp. 50–91). San Francisco: Jossey-Bass.

Brook, P. (1968). *The Empty Space.* New York: Atheneum.

Brunsson, K. (2007). *The Notion of General Management.* Malmö: Liber, Copenhagen Business School Press, and Universitetsforlaget.

Carlson, S. (1951). *Executive Behaviour: A Study of the Work Load and the Working Methods of Managing Directors.* Stockholm: Strombergs.

Carlson, S. (1991). *Executive Behaviour.* With comments by H. Mintzberg and R. Stewart. Uppsala: Uppsala University Press.

Carroll, G. R., & Teo, A. C. (1996). On the Social Network of Managers. *Academy of Management Journal, 39*(2), 421–440.

Charam, R., & Colvin, G. (1999). Why CEOs Fail. *Fortune,* June 21, pp. 30–40. Available: http://money.cnn.com/magazines/fortune/fortune_archive/1999/06/21/261696/

Clifford, P., & Friesen, S. L. (1993). A Curious Plan: Managing on the Twelfth. *Harvard Educational Review, 63*(3), 339–358.

Dalton, M. (1959). *Men Who Manage: Fusions of Feeling and Theory in Administration.* New York: Wiley.

Daudelin, M. W. (1996). Learning from Experience Through Reflection. *Organizational Dynamics, 24*(3), 36–48.

DePree, M. (1990). Today's Leaders Look to Tomorrow. *Fortune,* March 26, p. 30.

Drucker, P. F. (1946). *Concept of the Corporation.* New York: Day.

Drucker, P. F. (1954). *Practice of Management.* New York: Harper & Row.

Drucker, P. F. (1974). *Management: Tasks, Responsibilities, Practices.* New York: Harper & Row.

Ewing, D. W. (1990), *Inside the Harvard Business School: Strategies and Lessons of America's Leading School of Business.* New York: Crown.

Farson, R. E. (1996). *Management of the Absurd: Paradoxes in Leadership.* New York: Simon & Schuster.

Fayol, Henri. (1916). Administration industrielle et générale. *Bulletin de la Société de l'Industrie Minérale, 10,* 5–164.

Fayol, H. (1949). *General and Industrial Management.* London: Pitman.

Follett, M. P. (1920). *The New State: Group Organization the Solution of Popular Governments.* New York: Longmans Green.

Goleman, D. (2000). Leadership That Gets Results. *Harvard Business Review,* March–April, pp. 78–90.

Gosling, J., & Mintzberg, H. (2003). Five Minds of a Manager. *Harvard Business Review, 81*(11), 54–63.

Gowin, E. B. (1920). *The Executive and His Control of Men: A Study in Personal Efficiency.* New York: Macmillan.

Greenleaf, R. K. (2002). *Servant Leadership: A Journey into the Nature of Legitimate Power and Greatness* (25th anniversary ed.). New York: Paulist Press.

Grove, A. S. (1983). *High Output Management.* New York: Random House.

Guest, R. H. (1955–1956). Of Time and the Foreman. *Personnel, 32,* 478–486.

Hales, C. (1986). What Do Managers Do? A Critical Review of the Evidence. *Journal of Management Studies, 23*(1), 88–115.

Hales, C. (2001). Does It Matter What Managers Do? *Business Strategy Review, 12*(2), 50–58.

Hamel, G. (2000). Waking Up IBM: How a Gang of Unlikely Rebels Transformed Big Blue. *Harvard Business Review, 78* (July–August), 37–144.

Handy, C. B. (1994). *The Age of Paradox.* Boston: Harvard Business School Press.

Helgesen, S. (1990). *The Female Advantage: Women's Ways of Leadership.* New York: Doubleday/Currency.

Hill, L. A. (2003). *Becoming a Manager: How New Managers Master the Challenges of Leadership* (2nd, expanded ed.). Boston: Harvard Business School Press.

Hill, L. A. (2007). Becoming the Boss. *Harvard Business Review, 85* (January), 49–56.

Hodgson, R. C., Levinson, D. J., & Zaleznik, A. (1965). *The Executive Role Constellation: An Analysis of Personality and Role Relations in Management.* Cambridge, MA: Harvard Business School Press.

Hopwood, B. (1981). *Whatever Happened to the British Motorcycle Industry?* San Leandro, CA: Haynes.

Huy, Q. N. (2001). In Praise of Middle Managers. *Harvard Business Review, 79*(8), 72–79.

Iacocca, L., Taylor, A., III, & Bellis, W. (1988). Iacocca in His Own Words. *Fortune,* August 29, pp. 38–43.

Ives, B., & Olson, M. (1981). Manager or Technician? The Nature of the Information Systems Manager's Job. *MIS Quarterly, 5*(4), 49–63.

Kaplan, A. (1964). *The Conduct of Inquiry: Methodology for Behavioral Science.* San Francisco: Chandler.

Kotter, J. P. (1990). What Leaders Really Do. *Harvard Business Review, 68*(3), 103–111.

Kraut, A. I., Pedigo, P. R., McKenna, D. D., & Dunnette, M. D. (2005). The Role of the Manager: What's Really Important in Different Management Jobs. *Academy of Management Executive, 19*(4), 122–129.

Lewin, D. (1979). On the Place of Design in Engineering. *Design Studies, 1*(2), 113–117.

Lewis, J. M., Beavers, W. R., Gossett, J. T., & Phillips, V. A. (1976). *No Single Thread: Psychological Health in Family Systems*. New York: Brunner/Mazel.

Lindblom, C. E. (1968). *The Policy-Making Process*. Englewood Cliffs, NJ: Prentice Hall.

Livingston, J. S. (1971). Myth of the Well-Educated Manager. *Harvard Business Review, 49* (January–February), 79–89.

Maeterlinck, M. (1901). *The Life of the Bee*. New York: Dodd, Mead.

Maltz, M. D. (1997). *Bridging Gaps in Police Crime Data: Executive Summary*. Discussion Paper, BJS Fellow Program, Bureau of Justice Statistics. Washington, DC: U.S. Department of Justice, Office of Justice Programs.

McCall, M. W., Jr. (1988). Developing Executives through Work Experiences. *Human Resources Planning, 11*(1), 1–11.

McCall, M. W., Jr., Lombardo, M. M., & Morrison, A. M. (1988). *The Lessons of Experience: How Successful Executives Develop on the Job*. Lexington, MA: Lexington.

McCall, M. W., Jr., Morrison, A. M., & Hannan, R. L. (1978). *Studies of Managerial Work: Results and Methods* (Vol. 9, May). Greensboro, NC: Center for Creative Leadership.

McLuhan, H. M. (1962). *The Gutenberg Galaxy: The Making of Typographic Man*. Toronto: Toronto University Press.

Meindl, J. R., Ehrlich, S. B., & Dukerich, J. M. (1985). The Romance of Leadership. *Administrative Science Quarterly, 30,* 78–102.

Miller, D. (1990). *The Icarus Paradox*. New York: HarperCollins.

Miller, G. A. (1956). The Magic Number Seven, Plus or Minus Two: Some Limits on Our Capacity for Processing Information. *Psychological Review, 63,* 81–97.

Mintzberg, H. (1973). *The Nature of Managerial Work*. New York: Harper & Row.

Mintzberg, H. (1979). *The Structuring of Organizations: A Synthesis of the Research*. Englewood Cliffs, NJ: Prentice Hall.

Mintzberg, H. (1983). *Structure in Fives: Designing Effective Organizations*. Englewood Cliffs, NJ: Prentice Hall.

Mintzberg, H. (1987). Crafting Strategy. *Harvard Business Review,* *65*(4), 66–75.

Mintzberg, H. (1989). *Mintzberg on Management: Inside Our Strange World of Organizations.* New York: Free Press.

Mintzberg, H. (1990). Manager's Job: Folklore and Fact. *Harvard Business Review, 4,* 86–98.

Mintzberg, H. (1991). Managerial Work: Forty Years Later. In S. Carlson, *Executive Behaviour.* Uppsala: Uppsala University Press.

Mintzberg, H. (1994a). The Fall and Rise of Strategic Planning. *Harvard Business Review, 72*(1), 10.

Mintzberg, H. (1994b). Managing as Blended Care. *Journal of Nursing Administration, 24*(9), 29–36.

Mintzberg, H. (1994c). *The Rise and Fall of Strategic Planning: Reconceiving Roles for Planning, Plans, Planners.* New York: Free Press.

Mintzberg, H. (1994dc). Rounding Out the Manager's Job. *Sloan Management Review, 36*(1), 11–26.

Mintzberg, H. (1998). Covert Leadership. *Harvard Business Review, 76*(6), 140–147.

Mintzberg, H. (2004). *Managers, Not MBAs: A Hard Look at the Soft Practice of Managing and Management Development.* San Francisco: Berrett-Koehler.

Mintzberg, H. (2007). *Tracking Strategies: Toward a General Theory.* New York: Oxford University Press.

Mintzberg, H. (2009). *Managing.* San Francisco: Berrett-Koehler.

Mintzberg, H. (2011a). From Management Development to Organization Development with IMpact. *OD Practitioner, 43*(3).

Mintzberg, H. (2011b). Looking Forward to Development *Training & Development,* February 13.

Mintzberg, H. (2012). Developing Naturally: From Management to Organization to Society to Selves. In S. Snook, N. Nohria, & R. Khurana (Eds.), *The Handbook for Teaching Leadership: Knowing, Doing, and Being.* Thousand Oaks, CA: Sage.

Mintzberg, H., Simons, R., & Basu, K. (2002). Beyond Selfishness. *Sloan Management Review, 44,* 67–74.

Mintzberg, H., Ahlstrand, B., & Lampel, J. (2009). *Strategy Safari: A Guided Tour Through the Wilds of Management.* New York: Free Press.

Mintzberg, H., & Todd, P. (2012). The Offline Executive. *Strategy+Business,* Winter.

Morris, V. C., Crowson, R. L., Hurwitz, E., Jr., & Porter-Gehrie, C. (1981). *The Urban Principal. Discretionary Decision-Making in a Large Educational Organization.* Chicago: University of Illinois Press.

Morris, V. C., Crowson, R. L., Hurwitz, E., Jr., & Porter-Gehrie, C. (1982). The Urban Principal: Middle Manager in the Education Bureaucracy. *Phi Delta Kappan, 64*(10), 689–692.

Neustadt, R. E. (1960). *Presidential Power: The Politics of Leadership.* New York: Wiley.

Noël, A. (1989). Strategic Cores and Magnificent Obsessions: Discovering Strategy Formation Through Daily Activities of CEOs. *Strategic Management Journal, 10*(1), 33–49.

Peter, L. J., & Hull, R. (1969). *The Peter Principle.* New York: Morrow.

Peters, T. J. (1979). Leadership: Sad Facts and Silver Linings. *Harvard Business Review,* November–December, pp. 164–172.

Peters, T. J. (1990). *The Case for Experimentation: Or, You Can't Plan Your Way to Unplanning a Formerly Planned Economy.* Boston: TPG Communications.

Peters, T. J., & Waterman, R. H. (1982). *In Search of Excellence: Lessons from America's Best-Run Companies.* New York: Harper & Row.

Pitcher, P. C. (1995). *Artists, Craftsmen and Technocrats: The Dreams, Realities and Illusions of Leadership.* Toronto: Stoddart.

Pitcher, P. C. (1997). *The Drama of Leadership.* New York: Wiley.

Porter, M. E. (1987). Corporate Strategy: The State of Strategic Thinking. *The Economist,* May 23, pp. 17–22.

Rotman School of Management. (ca. 2005). *The Origin of Leaders.* Pamphlet, University of Toronto Press.

Sayles, L. R. (1964). *Managerial Behavior: Administration in Complex Organizations.* New York: McGraw-Hill.

Sayles, L. R. (1979). *Leadership: What Effective Managers Really Do . . . and How They Do It.* New York: McGraw-Hill.

Simons, R. (1995). *Levers of Control: How Managers Use Innovative Control Systems to Drive Strategic Renewal.* Boston: Harvard Business School Press.

Skinner, W., & Sasser, W. E. (1977). Managers with Impact: Versatile and Inconsistent. *Harvard Business Review, 55*(6), 140–148.

Stewart, R. (1967). *Managers and Their Jobs.* London: Macmillan.

Taylor, F. W. (1916). *The Principles of Scientific Management.* New York: Harper.

Tengblad, S. (2006). Is There a New Managerial Work? A Comparison with Henry Mintzberg's Classic Study 30 Years Later. *Journal of Management Studies, 43*(7), 1437–1461.

Thompson, J. D. (1967). *Organizations in Action: Social Science Bases of Administrative Theory.* New York: McGraw-Hill.

Weick, K. E. (1980). The Management of Eloquence. *Executive, 6*(3), 18–21.

Whyte, W. F. (1955). *Street Corner Society.* Chicago. University of Chicago Press.

Wilson, E. O. (1971). *The Insect Societies.* Cambridge, MA: Belknap.

Wrapp, H. E. (1967). Good Managers Don't Make Police Decisions. *Harvard Business Review, 45*(5), 91–99.

Zaleznick, A. (1977). Managers and Leaders: Are They Different? *Harvard Business Review,* May–June, pp. 67–78. (Reprint: *Harvard Business Review,* 2004, *82*(1), 74–81.)

Index

About the Author

In 1979, Henry Mintzberg published *The Structuring of Organizations*, in 512 pages. In 1983, he published these ideas in about half the length, under the title *Structure in Fives*. It became the best seller of his sixteen books. (Others of his books include *Managers Not MBAs* [2004], *Mintzberg on Management* [1989], and *The Rise and Fall of Strategic Planning* [1994].)

In 2009, he published *Managing. Simply Managing* is also about half that length. It is so titled not because managing is simple, or became simpler since 2009, but because both books are about managing, pure and simple. (The title for this book came up when Peter Todd, the dean of McGill's faculty of Management, described *Managing* in a reception on its publication as "simply managing.")

After studying mechanical engineering at McGill University, Henry worked in Operational Research at the Canadian National Railways before receiving his Master of Science and PhD degrees from the Sloan School of Management, MIT. He has been at the McGill University faculty of Management ever since—in recent years as Cleghorn Professor of Management Studies—aside from visiting professorships at the London Business School, Insead, and other schools.

Henry has received awards from prominent academic and practitioner associations, including the Academy of Management, the Strategic Management Society, and the Association of Management Consulting Firms. He was the first person from a management faculty named to the Royal Society of Canada and is an Officer of the Order of Canada and l'Ordre national du Québec. Eighteen universities around the world have granted him honorary degrees.

For the past two decades, he has been working with colleagues from McGill and elsewhere on a family of programs in which managers learn by reflecting in small groups on their own experience. These include the International Masters in Practicing Management (www.impm.org), the International Masters for Health Leadership (www.imhl.info), and the Advanced Leadership Program (www.impm-alp.com). These led to the establishment of www.CoachingOurselves.com, which enables groups of managers to learn in this way, and drive change, in their own workplace.

Henry is completing a monograph entitled "Managing the Myths of Health Care" and is now devoting his writing time to a set of "electronic pamphlets" under the title *Rebalancing Society: Radical Renewal beyond Left, Right, and Center.* Each is to be posted on www.mintzberg.org before being published in other forms. He continues to spend much of his personal time escaping organizations, on skates, skis, boots, and bikes, as well as in his canoe, most often in the Canadian wilderness.

Berrett–Koehler
Publishers

Berrett-Koehler is an independent publisher dedicated to an ambitious mission: *Creating a World That Works for All.*

We believe that to truly create a better world, action is needed at all levels—individual, organizational, and societal. At the individual level, our publications help people align their lives with their values and with their aspirations for a better world. At the organizational level, our publications promote progressive leadership and management practices, socially responsible approaches to business, and humane and effective organizations. At the societal level, our publications advance social and economic justice, shared prosperity, sustainability, and new solutions to national and global issues.

A major theme of our publications is "Opening Up New Space." Berrett-Koehler titles challenge conventional thinking, introduce new ideas, and foster positive change. Their common quest is changing the underlying beliefs, mindsets, institutions, and structures that keep generating the same cycles of problems, no matter who our leaders are or what improvement programs we adopt.

We strive to practice what we preach—to operate our publishing company in line with the ideas in our books. At the core of our approach is stewardship, which we define as a deep sense of responsibility to administer the company for the benefit of all of our "stakeholder" groups: authors, customers, employees, investors, service providers, and the communities and environment around us.

We are grateful to the thousands of readers, authors, and other friends of the company who consider themselves to be part of the "BK Community." We hope that you, too, will join us in our mission.

A BK Business Book

This book is part of our BK Business series. BK Business titles pioneer new and progressive leadership and management practices in all types of public, private, and nonprofit organizations. They promote socially responsible approaches to business, innovative organizational change methods, and more humane and effective organizations.

Berrett–Koehler
Publishers

A community dedicated to creating
a world that works for all

Visit Our Website: www.bkconnection.com

Read book excerpts, see author videos and Internet movies, read
our authors' blogs, join discussion groups, download book apps, find
out about the BK Affiliate Network, browse subject-area libraries of
books, get special discounts, and more!

Subscribe to Our Free E-Newsletter, the *BK Communiqué*

Be the first to hear about new publications, special discount offers,
exclusive articles, news about bestsellers, and more! Get on the list
for our free e-newsletter by going to **www.bkconnection.com**.

Get Quantity Discounts

Berrett-Koehler books are available at quantity discounts for orders
of ten or more copies. Please call us toll-free at (800) 929-2929 or
email us at bkp.orders@aidcvt.com.

Join the BK Community

BKcommunity.com is a virtual meeting place where people from
around the world can engage with kindred spirits to create a world
that works for all. BKcommunity.com members may create their own
profiles, blog, start and participate in forums and discussion groups,
post photos and videos, answer surveys, announce and register for
upcoming events, and chat with others online in real time. Please join
the conversation!

MIX
From responsible
sources
FSC® C113845
www.fsc.org

Certified

B

Corporation
bcorporation.net